IN-LAW RELATIONSHIPS

The Chapman Guide to
Becoming Friends with Your In-Laws

GARY D. CHAPMAN, PH.D.

TYNDALE HOUSE PUBLISHERS, INC.
Carol Stream, Illinois

Visit Tyndale's exciting Web site at www.tyndale.com

TYNDALE and Tyndale's quill logo are registered trademarks of Tyndale House Publishers, Inc.

In-Law Relationships: The Chapman Guide to Becoming Friends with Your In-Laws

Designed by Ron Kaufmann

Edited by Kathryn S. Olson

Library of Congress Cataloging-in-Publication Data

Chapman, Gary D., date.
  In-law relationships : the Chapman guide to becoming friends with your in-laws / Gary D. Chapman.
      p. cm.
  Includes bibliographical references and index.
  ISBN-13: 978-1-4143-0019-1 (hc : alk. paper)
  ISBN-10:1-4143-0019-0 (hc : alk. paper)
  1. Family—Religious aspects—Christianity.   2. Parents-in-law—Family relationships.   I. Title.
BT707.7.C53 2008
646.7'8—dc22   2008012508

Printed in the United States of America

14   13   12   11   10   09   08
 7   6   5   4   3   2   1

TABLE OF CONTENTS

Introduction

For thirty years, people have sat in my office and shared their struggles with in-laws. I have listened as they said:

- "My sister-in-law is driving me crazy. She is telling me how to raise my children, but she's single! What does she know about parenting?"

- "My mother-in-law and sisters-in-law exclude me. They have breakfast out each Saturday and never invite me to join them. They know that my mom and sisters live six hundred miles away. I feel left out of their girl things."

- "When my father-in-law comes to dinner, all he can talk about is sports, his work, or what he reads in the paper. He never asks about the details of our lives and seems to be totally disconnected from us emotionally."

- "My brother-in-law tries to control my husband. He is five years older and maybe he has done this all his life, but I don't like it."

- "Our son-in-law has essentially kidnapped our daughter. Since their marriage, he refuses to let her come to family events."

- "When my in-laws invite us to their home, they always include all their children and their families. Just once I wish they would have us over as a couple."

- "My wife's parents give her money to buy things we can't afford. I resent that. I wish they would let us run our own lives."

- "My husband's mother wants to tell me how to cook. I cooked my own meals for five years before we married. I think I know how to cook. I don't need her help."

🐦 "It's awkward to invite just my brother-in-law and sister-in-law to do things. My mother-in-law is divorced, and we feel pressure to include her."

🐦 "My husband's parents just 'drop in' unannounced. Sometimes I'm in the middle of a project I need to complete. I wish they would respect our schedule."

Perhaps you could add a few of your own complaints. In-law problems often focus on such issues as control, interference, inconvenience, and the clashing of values and traditions. The purpose of this book is to provide practical ideas on how to work through these struggles and build positive relationships.

When two people marry, they don't simply marry each other; they marry into an extended family consisting of mother-in-law, father-in-law, and perhaps sister-in-law and brother-in-law. These in-laws come in all sizes, shapes, and personalities. They come with a history of family traditions and ways of relating to one another. Whatever else we say about families, we can agree that all families are different. These differences often lead to adjustment difficulties.

If we are able to make these adjustments, we can create positive in-law relationships. If we don't, in-laws can be extremely troublesome. Parental relationships—his and hers—are the most common area of in-law conflicts.

In God's plan, in-laws were not designed to be divisive. They were meant to be supportive. Freedom and harmony are the biblical ideals for in-law relationships. In order to accomplish this ideal, marriages must run on the parallel tracks of separation from parents and devotion to parents.

SEPARATION FROM PARENTS

The Scriptures say, "For this reason a man will leave his father and mother and be united to his wife, and they will become one flesh."[1] God's pattern for marriage involves the "leaving" of parents and the "uniting" of husband and wife. Thus, marriage involves a change of allegiance. Before marriage,

one's allegiance is to parents. After marriage, the allegiance shifts to the mate.

We often call this "cutting the psychological apron strings." If there is a conflict of interest between a man's wife and his mother, the husband is to stand with his wife. This does not mean that the mother is to be treated unkindly; it does mean that she is no longer the dominant female in his life. The principle of separating from parents is extremely important. We will seek to apply this principle in the chapters that follow. No couple will reach their full potential in marriage without this psychological break from parents.

Perhaps nowhere is this principle of separation from parents more important than in decision making. Your parents and in-laws may have suggestions about many aspects of your married life. Each suggestion should be considered seriously, but in the final analysis you must make your own decisions. You must not allow parents to manipulate you into making decisions with which the two of you do not agree.

DEVOTION TO PARENTS

The second fundamental principle of marriage is that we are to honor our parents. God gave to ancient Israel the Ten Commandments, one of which is, "Honor your father and your mother, so that you may live long in the land the LORD your God is giving you."[2] In the New Testament, the apostle Paul affirmed this principle: "'Honor your father and mother'—which is the first commandment with a promise—'that it may go well with you and that you may enjoy long life on the earth.'"[3]

The command to honor parents does not cease when we are married. The word *honor* means to "show respect." It involves treating others with kindness and dignity. One wife said, "My parents do not live respectable lives. How can I respect them when I don't agree with what they are doing?" It is true that not all parents live honorable lives. Their actions may not be worthy of respect. But because they are made in the image of God and because they gave us life, we are to honor them. We may not agree with their lifestyle choices, but we can respect them as people even when we don't respect their behavior. It is always right to honor our parents and the parents of our spouse. Leaving parents for the purpose of marriage does not erase the responsibility to honor them.

How do we express honor to our parents in daily life? We honor them by keeping the lines of communication open—visiting, telephoning, and sending e-mails. In such communication, you are seeking to convey the message, "I still love you and want you to be a part of my life." *Leaving* must never be interpreted as *deserting*. Regular contact is a part of what it means to honor parents. Failure to communicate says in effect, "I no longer care."

Another way of honoring parents is described in the New Testament: "If a widow has children or grandchildren, these should learn first of all to put their religion into practice by caring for their own family and so repaying their parents and grandparents, for this is pleasing to God."[4] When we were young, our parents met our physical needs. As they grow older, we may have to do the same for them. If and when the need arises, we must bear the responsibility of caring for the physical needs of our parents. To fail in this responsibility is to deny our faith in Christ. Paul the apostle said, "If anyone does not provide for his relatives, and especially for his immediate family, he has denied the faith and is worse than an unbeliever."[5] By our actions, we must demonstrate our faith in Christ by honoring our parents.

FROM THE PARENTS' PERSPECTIVE

If we are the parents of married children, it will help if we remember our objective. Since their birth, we have been training our children for independence—or at least, we should have been doing so. We have taught them how to cook meals, wash dishes, make beds, buy clothes, save money, and make responsible decisions. We have taught them respect for authority and the value of the individual. In short, we have sought to bring them to maturity. We want them to be able to make it on their own.

At the time of their marriage, our goal of helping them become independent reaches fruition. We have helped them move from a state of complete dependence on us as infants to complete independence as newlyweds. In the future, we must view them as adults who will chart their own course, for better or for worse. We must never again impose our will upon them. We must respect them as equals.

This does not mean that we will no longer help our married children. It does mean that when we have a desire to help, we will ask first if they want our help. An unwanted gift is not a gift but a burden. Parents sometimes give financial aid to their married children, thus helping them to establish a standard of living they cannot afford. This practice does not foster independence. Neither should parents use gifts to influence a married child. "We will buy you a new car if you will . . ." is not a gift but an effort to manipulate.

Parents sometimes want to give advice to their married children. The rule of thumb is that parents should give advice only when requested. If your children have not requested your wisdom and you feel strongly urged to share it, at least ask permission. "Would you like for me to share my perspective on that?" is a good question. Giving unsolicited advice to your married children does not develop positive relationships.

The ideals to which we aspire are freedom and harmony. The married couple needs the emotional warmth that comes from a wholesome relationship with both sets of parents. Parents need the emotional warmth that comes from the couple. Life is too short to live with broken relationships. We will not always agree with our married children, but we can offer respect and give them the freedom to make their own decisions.

So how, exactly, do we become friends with our in-laws? In the next few pages, I'm going to share seven principles that will radically change in-law relationships.

I have intentionally kept this book brief because I know you are busy. You can probably read it in less than two hours. You will find that reading this book is a good investment of your time. At the end of each short chapter are practical suggestions on how to weave these ideas into the fabric of your own family life.

Whether you are the son-in-law, daughter-in-law, mother-in-law, father-in-law, sister-in-law, or brother-in-law, these principles are for you. If you will seek to apply these principles to your in-law relationships, I predict that you will begin to see positive changes in the attitudes and behavior of your in-laws. At the end of each chapter you will find a section entitled "Putting the Principles into Practice." Follow these suggestions and you will be on the road to positive in-law relationships.

1

*M*arsha's mother-in-law is affluent. Marsha, in contrast, grew up in a modest home where the emphasis was on self-sacrifice and giving. Her father was the chairman of the missions committee in their church, and her mother was actively involved in the women's ministry. Every year for as long as Marsha could remember, she had watched her parents save so they could give a significant gift to the annual missions offering. She herself had taken money out of her allowance as a child to give to this offering.

After two years of marriage, Marsha is totally frustrated with her mother-in-law. "Every month, she invites me to lunch. I'm always happy to see her. But after lunch, she insists on taking me shopping in order to buy me a new dress. At first I appreciated her generosity, but as time went on, it seemed like our lunches got shorter and shorter while our shopping sprees extended into the afternoon. She never looks for dresses on sale, and she has bought me some really expensive dresses."

Marsha continued, "I see it as an extravagant waste of money, and I feel like she is trying to buy my friendship. When I tell her that I don't need a dress this month, she says, 'Every lady needs a new dress. It lifts the spirit.'

"Well, it's not lifting my spirits," said Marsha. "It's making me resent her. Why doesn't she give that money to people who really need it? My closet is full of dresses. I don't want to hurt her feelings. I'd like for us to have a relationship that does not focus on shopping. I'd like to have a nice, quiet, extended lunch with her. I'd like to know what her childhood was like . . . what kind of struggles she and my father-in-law had in the early years of their marriage . . . how she felt about being a stay-at-home mom. All she ever talks about is her golf game and her bridge parties. I sometimes get the feeling that she's extremely lonely and that shopping is her way of trying to forget her loneliness. I don't know. I just wish our relationship could be more real."

All these thoughts and feelings Marsha had kept to herself. She tried to share them with her husband, Rob, but his response was, "Let Mom buy you dresses. It's her way of showing you that she loves you." Perhaps Rob was right, but if so, his mother is missing the mark. Marsha does not feel loved; she feels resentful.

"Have you tried to share any of these thoughts and feelings with your mother-in-law?" I asked.

"Not really," Marsha responded. "She's so overpowering. She talks most of the time and seldom asks me a question; when she does, I have the sense that she's not listening to my response. She's thinking about what she's going to say next. I feel tense when I'm around her."

It was obvious to me that Marsha had a mother-in-law problem, and it wasn't going away unless Marsha took some initiative.

"But I can't just tell her that I resent her," said Marsha. "And I can't stop having lunches with her. That's our only contact. If I tell her I don't want the dresses, I'm afraid she'll be hurt. I really don't know what to do. That's why I'm here."

"I'm glad you came," I said. "I'm not a miracle worker, but I do have an idea that I would like to suggest. The next time you have lunch with your mother-in-law, say to her, 'Before we go shopping, I want to ask you a question. On a scale of one to ten, how much pleasure do you get out of taking me shopping?' If her answer is eight, nine, or ten (which is what I would expect), then you ask, 'Tell me why you get so much pleasure out of being nice to me.'

"Listen to her answer carefully. Then tell her what you think you heard her say and ask her if that is correct. For example, you might say, 'What I hear you saying is that you enjoy buying things for me because when you were first married, your mother-in-law did nothing for you and you felt hurt. You didn't want that to happen in our relationship. Is that correct?' Continue to ask clarifying questions until you feel that you understand what is behind her desire to take you shopping.

"Then express appreciation to her for what she is doing for you. Once you understand her motivation, I think you will find that easier to do. Tell her that you really appreciate her being so kind and thoughtful of you. Then tell her how meaningful this conversation has been to you: that you feel like you know her better, and you appreciate her even more. Then go shopping with her and let her buy you whatever she wishes.

"The next month when you have lunch, ask your mother-in-law additional questions. Tell her how much you enjoyed your conversation with her last month and that if she doesn't mind, you'd like to ask her some more questions about her life. You might ask such questions as 'What was it like growing up as a child in your house?' 'What was high school like for you?' 'How did you meet your husband?' 'What made you decide to get married?'

'What were the early years in your marriage like?' 'What have been some of the things you have enjoyed most about your marriage and family?' These are probably too many questions for one conversation, but pick and choose.

"What you are trying to do is to get to know your mother-in-law better. We do this by asking questions and listening to answers. Again, ask clarifying questions to make sure you understand what she is saying. For example, 'It sounds like you had a lot of hurt from your father's behavior. Is that correct?' Whatever you hear her say, repeat it in the form of a question to give her an opportunity to clarify. Tell her how much you are enjoying the conversation and that you appreciate her willingness to share her story. Then go shopping.

"When she calls the third month and invites you to lunch, you say to her, 'I can't wait to see you. I enjoyed our conversation so much last time. I have a suggestion. I've been wanting to go to the new art exhibit downtown. What if, after lunch, we go see the art exhibit instead of going shopping?' If she accepts your suggestion, great. If, on the other

hand, she says, 'Why don't we go to the art exhibit *and* go shopping,' you say to her, 'Well, maybe we would have time to do that, but could we do the art exhibit first and then play it by ear?' Chances are, she'll agree. After you have gone to the art exhibit, the two of you can decide whether or not you have time to go shopping. Maybe you can do a quick shopping trip this time or not go shopping at all. Either way, you have changed the typical pattern of lunch and shopping.

"The fourth month, you can engage her in another meaningful conversation and make the suggestion that perhaps in the future you could rotate between shopping one month and doing some other social activity together the following month. You might say 'After all, my closet is getting full, and I really enjoy doing other things with you.' If she accepts your proposal, you have now changed the paradigm of the monthly shopping trip.

"In future months, you can be brave enough to suggest that perhaps this month, instead of buying things for you, 'We can take my friend's adopted Chinese daughter and buy clothes for her.' Or another month, perhaps you can buy groceries for a needy family or school supplies for a group of students from low-income families. Little by little, you will be helping your mother-in-law channel her giving into areas that both of you feel good about. And you will be getting to know your mother-in-law as a person, not as simply a lady with whom you have lunch and go shopping."

At the end of our conversation, Marsha was elated. She said to me, "If half of what you have described could come true in my relationship with my mother-in-law, I would be extremely happy."

Over the coming months, Marsha saw most of these visions turn into reality. She and her mother-in-law became best friends. She learned to accept her mother-in-law's gifts as expressions of love, and she taught her mother-in-law how to share life on a deeper level. Some months later, I met the mother-in-law in a social setting. She said to me, "Marsha is the best thing that ever happened in my life. Having a son is great, but having a daughter-in-law is even better." I don't know how her son would feel about that, but it is evident that she has a genuine fondness for Marsha.

Marsha's story demonstrates the power of listening. The purpose of listening is to discover what is going on inside the minds and emotions of other people. If we understand why people do what they do, we can have more appropriate responses. For example, Marsha's whole attitude toward her mother-in-law changed when she discovered that her mother-in-law's motivation for buying her dresses was because, in the early years of her marriage, she had very little money for clothes and was often embarrassed about her wardrobe. Understanding often changes our perception of people and, consequently, our negative emotions toward them.

It is a fundamental psychological principle that we cannot read other people's minds. We observe their behavior, but we do not know what is behind the behavior until we listen. Most of us have not been trained to listen. Consequently, we often misunderstand our in-laws. I want to share with you some guidelines for effective listening:

ASK QUESTIONS

The most effective way to find out what is going on in the minds of your in-laws is to ask questions. Most people do not communicate the thoughts and feelings that motivate their behavior unless they are asked. Marsha could readily observe the behavior of her mother-in-law (taking her shopping and buying her dresses), but she did not know that her mother-in-law's behavior was motivated by events that transpired in the early days of her own marriage. This information came only in response to a question.

Questions must be carefully crafted. The more specific the question, the more likely you are to receive the information you seek. You may ask preliminary questions simply to bring up the topic. For example, "Who do you think will win the pennant?" puts the topic of baseball on the table. Then you can ask, "When did you become interested in baseball? And what stimulated your interest?" The answers to these questions may let you know why your father-in-law never misses a baseball game.

Questions must always be sincere. You are not asking a series of questions in order to push your in-laws into a corner and win an argument. You are asking questions to try to understand them. When people sense that you are genuinely interested in them and want to know them better, they will typically answer your questions honestly and freely. Marsha's mother-in-law was not reluctant to talk about the early days of her marriage. Marsha had simply never expressed interest in that part of her life. When she saw that Marsha was sincerely interested, she talked openly about what motivated her interest in shopping and gift giving.

Asking your in-laws to rate their feelings on a scale of one to ten is a quick and easy way to learn how strongly they feel about a particular subject. Jason used this technique in opening a discussion with his father-in-law. Jason was frustrated over his father-in-law's propensity for gambling. When he learned that his father-in-law had taken Jason's ten-year-old son, Bobby, to the casino, Jason was livid and told his wife, "I will never let Bobby see your father again." Two weeks later, after he'd calmed down, I challenged Jason to ask questions and listen to his father-in-law's answers.

He asked his father-in-law, "On a scale of one to ten, how much do you enjoy going to the casino?" When his father-in-law said "ten," Jason knew this was something that was extremely important to him. Jason then followed up by asking, "Why do you think you gain so much pleasure from gambling?"

His father-in-law responded, "For me, it's recreation. I'm gambling because I have money and I don't have to worry about how I spend it. When I was a child, we had very little. We never knew if we would have a meal at dinner or whether my father would say, 'Let's go to bed early, and we'll have a big breakfast in the morning.' Breakfast was always oatmeal; we could have as much as we liked. I saw my friends at school with money to burn, and I determined that when I got to be an adult, I would make money and never have to ask anyone for anything. And I have. Now I can enjoy spending my money in any way I choose. If I lose a thousand dollars, so what? I can afford it."

"So for you," Jason continued, "it's not a matter of winning or losing; it's a matter of having fun."

His father-in-law responded, "It's not just fun. It's freedom; freedom to do what I want to with what I have."

"I think I can see what you're saying," said Jason. "I think all of us want to be free, and this is one way of expressing your freedom."

In a thousand years, Jason would never have guessed what was going on in the mind of his father-in-law, but two questions, accompanied by a listening ear, helped him understand his father-in-law's motivation. He still did not want Bobby going to the casino, but having heard and understanding his father-in-law, he was able to express his concerns in a constructive way. He shared his own understanding that many people who gamble are not free but are, in fact, enslaved by gambling and have lost not only recreational money but, indeed, all their financial assets. He explained his desire to keep Bobby from being exposed to something that had the potential for becoming addictive and destroying his freedom, and he requested that his father-in-law not take Bobby to the casino in the future. His father-in-law understood and agreed.

While both Marsha's and Jason's stories have "happy endings," I do not mean to imply that asking questions and understanding the motivation of our in-laws guarantees a satisfactory solution to the issues that trouble us. But by asking questions and listening empathetically, we are much more likely to find a resolution to these issues. And in the process we will be able to preserve—or even improve—our relationships with our in-laws.

DON'T INTERRUPT

When your in-laws are talking, the tendency is to interrupt if they say something with which you disagree. When you interrupt and give your perspective, you have taken the first step to a full-blown argument. Arguments are counterproductive. Someone wins and someone loses, and the issue is not resolved.

Remember when Marsha's mother-in-law said, "I think the reason I find so much pleasure in buying things for you is that in the first years of our marriage, we had little money and I often was embarrassed by the things I had to wear"? Suppose

Marsha had interrupted and said, "*We* have *plenty* of money. Rob has a good job. You don't need to buy me things." She would have entered into an argument that likely would have further damaged her relationship with her mother-in-law. Suppose Jason had interrupted his father-in-law and said, "That's a cop-out; I don't believe that for a moment. I think you gamble because you're addicted." He and his father-in-law would likely have had a shouting match that would have further fractured the relationship.

The purpose of listening is to understand, not to make a point. Our "point" will be made much later in the conversation. In the early stages, we are trying to understand what is going on in the mind and heart of an in-law so that we then can respond appropriately. Interruptions derail the process of understanding. For some people, refraining from interrupting will be extremely difficult. They have developed an argumentative pattern of communication. They listen only long enough to gather their own thoughts; then they interrupt and disagree with whatever the other person is saying. These individuals will never have a positive relationship with in-laws—or anyone else—until they learn to break the destructive pattern of argument. Relationships are built by seeking understanding. They are destroyed by interruptions and arguments.

If you have trouble continuing to listen to your in-laws when you disagree with what they are saying, let me suggest a mental image that may be helpful. When you have asked a question and your in-laws are talking, picture yourself with huge elephant ears on both sides of your face. The ears remind you "I'm a listener. I want to understand. I will not interrupt. I will have my chance to share my ideas later. Right now, I'm trying to listen to what my in-laws are saying. I want to know where they are coming from, and I want to understand how they view their behavior. I am trying to build a relationship, not make an enemy." Learning to listen without interrupting is a foundational step to effective listening.

CLARIFY MEANING

Even when we are consciously focusing on listening, we often misunderstand what another person is trying to communicate. We listen through our own earphones, which sometimes distort the meaning behind another person's words. We can clarify meaning by telling the person what we think they are saying and asking if we have heard them correctly. Jason demonstrated this when he said, "So for you, it's not a matter of winning or losing; it's a matter of having fun." This allowed his father-in-law to clarify by bringing up the idea of freedom. From this feedback, Jason was able to learn more about what was going on in his father-in-law's mind.

Some people object that clarifying questions seem to be rather mechanical. One husband said, "I get tired of saying 'What I hear you saying is . . .' And I'm sure other people must get tired of hearing it." It is true that the same response, couched in the same words, can become monotonous and annoying. However, clarifying questions can be asked in many ways. Here are some examples:

- "Is this what you are saying . . . ?"

- "Do you mean . . . ?"

- ☞ "I think I understand you. Tell me if I've got it right. . . ."

- ☞ "I think what I'm hearing is . . . Is that what you're saying?"

- ☞ "I want to make sure I understand. Are you saying . . . ?"

When we learn to ask clarifying questions in various ways, the questions become a part of the natural flow of our conversation. When an in-law responds, "Yes, you understand what I'm saying," then you will know he or she feels you've heard correctly. Then you're ready for the next step.

EXPRESS APPRECIATION

Once your in-law has told you that you understand what he or she has said, you may say, "I really appreciate your sharing that with me. I think I understand you better, and what you are saying makes a lot of sense." With that simple response, you are no longer an enemy. You have created a positive climate.

Affirming statements do not mean that you necessarily agree with what your in-laws have said. It does mean that you listened long enough to see the world through their eyes and to understand that, in their minds, what they are doing makes good sense. You are affirming their humanity, the right to think and feel differently from other people.

Some will ask, "How can you affirm what your in-laws are saying when you totally disagree with them?" My answer is: You are not necessarily affirming the validity of what they are saying. You are affirming their right to have this perspective. You are giving them the same freedom that God gives them. You are allowing them to be human.

Affirmation does not mean that you agree with their ideas or that you like their emotions. It means that you understand how they have come to hold their ideas and how they might feel the way they feel. Given their personalities and their perspectives on issues, it's not difficult to see how they could reach their conclusions and to understand their emotions.

I cannot overemphasize the value of expressing appreciation because it creates the climate for the next important step:

SHARE YOUR PERSPECTIVE

Now that you have asked questions, allowed your in-laws to speak without interruption, clarified meaning, and expressed appreciation, you are ready to share your perspective. Because you have taken the time to treat them with dignity and respect, they are far more likely to listen to your perspective.

When Jason shared with his father-in-law why he did not want Bobby to go to the casino, his father-in-law was willing to listen and agree. Had Jason not taken the time to first listen to his father-in-law, had he simply condemned the older man's behavior and told him that Bobby would never be allowed to go with him to the casino, their relationship might have remained fractured for a lifetime. It was the process of listening that brought them to a healthy conclusion.

When Marsha began to suggest alternatives to shopping, her mother-in-law was open to the alternatives because she sensed that Marsha genuinely wanted to have a good relationship with her. Had Marsha not expressed appreciation for her mother-in-law's willingness to share information from the early years of her own marriage, the mother-in-law might never have been open to Marsha's suggestions. When we express appreciation, we are more likely to be heard by our in-laws and to reach a satisfying solution.

Your perspective on the situation is also extremely important. You are one of the key players in this in-law relationship. You need to be heard; your ideas and feelings are important. Now that you have communicated a positive respect for your in-laws, you are ready to say, "Let me share my perspective with you. Here is what I'm struggling with. Here is my objective. Here is what I think is important." And you fully explain your perspective.

Because you have listened, you are far more likely to be listened to. Because you have not interrupted, you are less likely to be interrupted. Because you have clarified meaning, your in-laws are more likely to clarify meaning. Because you have expressed appreciation, they are more likely to express appreciation to you, and together, you can accept your differences and find healthy solutions.

In this chapter we have discussed the first step in becoming friends with your in-laws. Listening has brought you deeper understanding of each other, and understanding has led you to positive conclusions that will make the future easier for all of you. In the next chapter, we will look at the power of respect.

PUTTING THE PRINCIPLES INTO PRACTICE

Choose an in-law relationship that you would like to improve, and think about this specific relationship as you consider the following questions:

1. What questions do you need to ask in order to better understand your in-law?

2. In your conversations, do you have a tendency to interrupt? If your answer is yes, what will you do to break this pattern?

3. Try using clarifying questions in your next conversation; for example, "Is this what you are saying?"

4. Read the following statement aloud three times: "I really appreciate your sharing that with me. I think I understand you better, and what you are saying makes a lot of sense." Look for an opportunity to use this statement with your in-law.

When you learn to ask good questions, clarify meaning, express appreciation, and refuse to interrupt, you will then be ready to say, "Let me share my perspective." Since you have listened to them, they will likely listen to you.

2

LEARN THE ART OF SHOWING RESPECT

*R*espect is a major ingredient in building positive in-law relationships. The word *respect* means "to consider worthy of esteem."[1] It has to do with the way we view people. For me, respect means that I choose to see you as being extremely important because you are made in God's image. My choice to respect you is not based on your character or on your treatment of me. Rather, it is based upon my perception of who you are.

Respect has nothing to do with the behavior of my in-laws or their opinion of themselves. They may see themselves as being the scum of society or as being God's gift to mankind. Thus, their view of themselves may be marred or exalted. Whatever their view of themselves, I view them as persons who have great value because they bear the image of the Creator.

I may not like their behaviors, but I respect them as being fellow humans. They are gifted by God with a level of intelligence, with the capacity to experience emotions, and with freedom of choice. Also, they are ultimately responsible to God for how they use their lives.

When I choose the attitude of respect, it will be reflected in my behavior. Respect leads me to give my in-laws the same freedom that God allows me and all humans—the freedom to be different. Therefore, I will not seek to impose my will upon my in-laws. Rather, when I find myself at odds with them, I will look for a solution that will show respect for our differences. I will not seek to control them, nor will I allow them to control me. I will give to them the same respect that I hope they will give to me.

I may well feel irritated by something my in-laws say or do. The feeling of irritation is not sinful; however, I am responsible for how I respond to my irritation. If I lash out with harsh or critical words, then I have sinned. I have failed to show respect. If, on the other hand, I treat them with dignity by seeking to understand their perspective and then looking for win-win solutions, I am showing respect.

In an effort to make this practical, let's look at five areas in which we commonly have opportunity to show respect to our in-laws.

RESPECTING HOLIDAY TRADITIONS

Marriage brings together two families, each of which has a history of celebrating holidays. It is inevitable that the manner in which they celebrate these holidays will be different. And the importance that they attach to these holiday celebrations will also differ from family to family.

For many young couples, the first Christmas becomes the first major conflict in the marriage. His mother wants the two of you at her house on

Christmas Day, while her mother has the same desire. That may be possible if the parents live in close proximity and one focuses their celebration around lunch and the other around dinner. However, if they live more than a hundred miles apart, this arrangement is not feasible. If one set of in-laws insists on your presence on Christmas Day and the other set of in-laws reluctantly acquiesces, you have planted the seeds of resentment. Respect is absent in this decision. The in-laws who demanded your presence are not respecting the desires of the other in-laws, nor are they respecting your freedom as a young couple to make your own decisions.

If the art of showing respect had been applied, what might have happened? Both sets of parents would have freely communicated their personal desires to have the couple on Christmas Day. When informed that both sets of parents had the same desire, they would have encouraged the young couple to think through the situation and suggest an alternate plan. The couple are now free to explore possibilities. The couple may decide to decline both invitations and spend Christmas Day with each other. If distance is not a problem, they may suggest that they spend Christmas Eve with one set of in-laws and Christmas Day with the other, with the understanding that the following year they would switch the sequence. If distance prohibits this dual visit, they may suggest Christmas with one set of in-laws this year and the other set of in-laws next year. Who is first could be determined by the flip of a coin. If one parent is critically ill, then this may be sufficient reason to choose to be with them the first Christmas. If time and money are not a problem, Thanksgiving Day may be put into the mix so that both parents would see the couple within the space of six weeks.

You can see that there are several equally work-able solutions to this holiday conflict. All of them require an attitude of respect from each of the fam-ily members. If respect is not present, then Christ-mas will not be a symbol of "peace on earth." I have known young couples who stayed away from both sets of in-laws at Christmas, not because they did not desire to be there, but because they felt that both sets of parents were trying to manipulate them.

Manipulation is the opposite of respect. Respect says, "This is what I would like and this is why I would like it. But I also know that you must make the decision that you believe is best for you." Respect always allows freedom of choice.

I have known couples who freely admitted that they both preferred to be with one set of in-laws during the holidays rather than the other. Typically, this is because the emotional climate in one setting is extremely stressful, perhaps because of alcohol, verbal abuse, or unresolved conflicts from the past. However, I encourage young couples not to allow these feelings to lead them to write off one set of in-laws.

The Scriptures say to "honor your father and your mother."[2] We do not honor parents by writing them off. We can be honest about our feelings, honest about the stress level that we experience when we are with them, but we must not allow these realities to control our behavior. We honor parents not because we believe they are honorable but because they gave us life. Without them, we would not be here. That is a huge debt. We honor them by considering the request of one set of in-laws in the same manner that we consider the request of the other set of in-laws. We may not approve of the lifestyle of one or both sets of in-laws. We may consider their behavior not worthy of esteem. But we esteem them as persons of worth because they bear the image of the Creator.

Of course, if there is drug and alcohol abuse, profane language, and verbal or physical abuse, then you certainly must take that into account in deciding whether or not to celebrate the holidays with them, especially if you have children. One approach is to respect their freedom to make these lifestyle choices but request that while you and your children are there for the holidays they refrain from these behaviors. If they choose to respect you in the same way that you are respecting them, they may well agree, and you can have a healthy celebration of the holidays.

SHOWING RESPECT FOR RELIGIOUS DIFFERENCES

Ours is truly a global society. The couple next door may be Buddhist; the couple down the street,

Hindu; the man who works with you, Muslim; and most of the rest, Christian. Within the Christian framework, there are many religious "dialects." There is the Methodist dialect, Presbyterian dialect, Baptist dialect, and so forth. Each of these dialects represents a different way of expressing and practicing the Christian faith. They all agree on a common core of Christian beliefs, but beyond that, they differ in many ways.

Most people come to marriage having grown up in a religious context. They may have deeply held personal religious beliefs, or they may treat the belief system in which they grew up rather lightly. They may even have rejected the religion or religions of their parents. Seldom do two individuals come to marriage with the same religious background and beliefs, even if they grew up in the same church. These religious differences often become divisive in the marriage. They can also create barriers to wholesome in-law relationships. I remember the Protestant couple who said, "Our daughter married a Catholic. When they were dating, he visited our church and told us that he was not strongly committed to the Catholic church. But when the children came along, he insisted that they be raised in his religion. We feel like he deceived our daughter. Consequently, we don't have a very good relationship with him."

Because religion is such a vital part of life, I strongly urge couples considering marriage to explore fully the religious foundation on which they are seeking to build their relationship. When differences on fundamental religious beliefs are greatly diverse, these issues need to be resolved before the marriage. Otherwise, they can become huge barriers to marital unity. However, even when the two of them agree on fundamental religious questions, they may find themselves in strong disagreement with their in-laws' religious perspective. One young husband said, "My sister married a Muslim. He told her that all religions were basically the same, but she soon realized that was not the case. It has been very difficult to build a positive relationship with my brother-in-law because he disagrees with almost everything I believe. Even if we try to stay away from the topic of religion, our fundamental religious beliefs tend to spill over onto the rest of life and we end up arguing about other issues as well."

It is true that when one is committed to a religious system of thought, it influences the way one views all of life. That is why the apostle Paul urged Christians not to marry non-Christians.[3] If we are going to have marital unity in the spiritual area of life, we must be close enough in our fundamental beliefs to be able to dialogue and grow together.

Because religious beliefs often go unexcavated in the dating phase of the relationship, couples often find themselves married before they realize that they have vastly different religious perspectives. These differences may be between the two of them or between them and their in-laws. So how do we process these differences, and what role does showing respect play?

Let's begin by admitting that we may never be able to resolve all our religious conflicts. Efforts at blending various religions have never been very effective. On the other hand, if we try to convince our in-laws that their religious beliefs are wrong, we will likely experience nonproductive arguments. However, if we begin with the choice to respect their religious beliefs, we create a platform on which we can have authentic dialogue. In this atmosphere, both sides can come to understand each other's beliefs more fully and even question each other's beliefs while respecting the other's right to believe what they choose.

Respect for your in-laws' religious beliefs is a foundational requirement for building positive in-law relationships. This does not mean that you will agree with their beliefs. It does mean that you will give them the same freedom of choice that God grants them. Not all religious beliefs could possibly be true, for many of these beliefs actually contradict the others. Typically, we believe that our own religious beliefs are true. However, your in-laws also have the same persuasion about their religious beliefs. Respecting an individual's freedom to choose is the foundation for all meaningful dialogue. With respect, we can have a meaningful, positive relationship even when we disagree on certain religious beliefs.

Eric and Jan were deeply committed Christians. He grew up in a Methodist home, and she grew up in a Presbyterian family. However, each of them made the discovery of a personal commitment to Jesus Christ while they were in college. They had believed the Christian faith while growing up, but their beliefs never profoundly affected their behavior. In a college classroom where the Christian faith was being questioned by an unbelieving professor, they were challenged to find answers to his attacks on the validity of the Christian faith. This pursuit led them to the personal conclusion that Jesus Christ was, indeed, divine; that his life from beginning to end gave evidence of supernatural power; and that his resurrection from the dead validated his teachings. They became involved in a Bible study group and began to invest their lives in reaching out to the troubled neighborhoods in their university town. They knew that when they finished college, their lives would never be the same.

When they got married shortly after graduation, they never anticipated that religion would be a point of conflict between them and their parents. Eric and Jan joined a community church. His father asked, "What denomination is the church?"

Eric replied, "It's not affiliated with any denomination; it's just a Christian church."

"How can it be a Christian church and not be associated with any denomination?"

"I don't know," Eric said. "I just know it's a church that teaches the Scriptures and people try to follow the teachings of Jesus. We like it and feel it's where we need to be."

"I don't know why you didn't join a Methodist church or a Presbyterian church. Why would you have to join a no-name church? It seems to me they must be hiding something. Are you sure it's not a cult?"

When Jan shared with her parents that they had joined the community church, she got a similar response. "I guess we just assumed that you and Eric would join a Presbyterian church or a Methodist church since that's what the two of you grew up in. I wish you had discussed it with us before you made your decision," her mother said. "Was this Eric's idea or your idea?"

"We both had the same idea, Mom. It's the church we believe God wants us to attend."

"I think you had better pray some more about that," her mother said as she walked out of the room.

Eric and Jan were shocked at their parents' responses. Some time later, they began to realize that her parents were blaming Eric for pulling Jan into a no-name church, and Eric's parents were blaming Jan. In time, religion became an "off-limits" topic with both in-laws, but this young couple had to live with the awareness that their parents disagreed with their choice of church.

When they came to my office for help, I was empathetic with their frustration. Over the past thirty years, I have encountered numerous couples who were in conflict with their parents/in-laws over religious differences.

"We really don't have that many differences," Eric said. "The basic teachings in our church are the same as in the church of my parents. It is true that our church has a more contemporary worship style and the members are more heavily involved in Bible study, prayer meetings, and getting outside the walls of the church to minister to the needs of the community. But we have the same fundamental beliefs. I don't understand why this has become such a problem with them." I listened carefully as Jan also shared her struggles with her parents and her in-laws.

"I'm glad you came," I said. "I'd hate to see you struggle with this frustration for the next twenty years. My guess is that your parents' opposition to your being a part of the community church is based on fear and love. They love both of you very much. They want you to have a productive life. Their churches have been an important part of their lives through the years, and they want that for you, too. Their fear is based on the unknown. They know what a Methodist church is, and they know what a Presbyterian church is. But they don't know about community churches. They are fearful that this might be a cultic Christian group that will pull you into beliefs and practices that are detrimental to your well being."

"But that's not true," said Eric.

"*I* know it's not true, but *they* don't know it's not true," I said. "All of us fear the unknown."

"So, how can we help them understand?" asked Jan.

"It all begins with respect," I said. "You must respect their choice of churches, and they must respect yours."

"We do respect their choices," Jan said, "but they don't respect ours."

"Let's hope that can change," I said.

"That's why we came," said Eric. "If they could just respect our choice and trust us the way we trust them, everything would be fine."

That was the first of several sessions I had with Eric and Jan. Within six months, they had won the respect of both sets of in-laws. The process began with an open conversation between Eric and Jan and his parents in which he was the spokesman. He shared with his parents that he and Jan really wanted to have harmony over his and Jan's choice of church and that he and Jan were willing to try to understand his parents' concerns but also wanted to share their own perspective.

He suggested that they begin by getting a list of the basic beliefs of the Methodist church, the Presbyterian church, and the community church and then compare those beliefs to see where there might or might not be genuine differences. "We really want to understand you, and we want you to understand us. We know that you love us and that you have our best interests in mind." His parents readily accepted this invitation.

The couple had a similar conversation with Jan's parents in which Jan was the spokeswoman. Her parents also were happy to discuss the matter.

When they actually compared the core beliefs of the three churches, all parties agreed that the basic beliefs were the same.

Eric also suggested that they would like to read a brief history of the Methodist church if his parents could secure it from their pastor. And Jan asked her parents for the same from the Presbyterian church. Both sets of parents agreed that they would like to read the history themselves. "The community church doesn't have much of a history," Eric said, "but we will find out how our church got started and share it with you." What they all discovered was that the motivation for starting the community church was quite similar to that of the early followers of John Wesley, who founded the Methodist church, and the followers of John Knox, who established the Presbyterian church.

In the meantime, Eric and Jan visited the Methodist church with his parents and the Presbyterian church with her parents, and each of the parents visited the community church with them. In the process, parental fears were allayed.

Eric and Jan expressed appreciation to their parents for being willing to explore the possibility that their choice of the community church was a wise choice for them. And before long, both sets of parents agreed. Now, from time to time, they visit one another's churches for special events. The parents have come to respect Eric and Jan's choice in much the same way as the young couple showed respect for the parents'.

Unfortunately, not all religious differences will be solved to this level of satisfaction. But this serves as an excellent model for how to go about addressing differences. Beginning with respect will always improve situations to some degree.

SHOWING RESPECT FOR PRIVACY

I was making a quick run to the grocery store for cereal and milk. As I made my turn into the cereal aisle, I encountered Tim and Marie. I recognized them as having attended a parenting class at which I had recently spoken. After we greeted each other, Tim said, "I know this is not the place for a counseling session, but we really need help with my mom and dad. They are driving us crazy. We don't want to hurt them, but we have got to do something."

"So, what's the situation?" I asked.

Marie responded, "We never know when they'll drop in for a visit. They never bother to call and tell us they're coming; they just show up at the door. Sometimes, it's very inconvenient. The children may be doing their homework, or I may be involved in doing laundry. I don't have time to sit down and talk with them, and the children need to get their homework done. The worst thing, and the reason we're so upset today . . ." Marie looked up at Tim, and he picked up the conversation.

"Last week, we had put the children to bed early so we could have some private time together, and just when we were about to make love, the doorbell rang and my folks walked in. As you can imagine, it destroyed our romantic evening together."

"It's just not fair," said Marie. "I'm beginning to resent them. I wish we had some scheduled times for them to visit when it is convenient for us."

"Have you talked with your folks about this?" I inquired.

Tim said, "I tried to, a couple of years ago. Mom got upset and didn't call or come by to visit for three weeks. Then all of a sudden, they showed up at our house one day as if nothing had happened. And they've been showing up ever since. We've never talked about it again."

"How often do they drop in?" I asked.

"At least once a week," Marie said, "and there's no pattern to when they show up. It can be any day, any time."

"Do you ever visit their house?" I asked.

"Yes," Tim said, "but we always call before we go. We thought that maybe our calling might give them the idea that it would be nice if they called us before they came. But obviously, this hasn't worked. In fact, Mom has told me, 'You don't have to call before you come. You can come any time. You're family.' I guess we have a different idea of what it means to be family."

"It sounds to me like the problem is lack of respect," I said. "Your parents are not respecting your privacy as a family."

"Exactly," Marie replied. "But what do we do about it?"

"Well, you don't gain respect by being disrespectful," I said. "So, what you don't want to do is to lose your temper and lash out at them in anger, tell them how inconsiderate they are, or inform them that you are sick and tired of their messing up your plans."

"So far we have not done that," Marie said, "but believe me, I have been tempted."

"I can understand that," I said, "but I think you can see that will only make things worse."

"I don't think it could get much worse," Marie said.

"Well, let's focus on trying to make it better," I replied. "You must talk with your parents about the problem. The passing of time will not bring a resolution. I think you've seen that."

They were both nodding and saying, "Yes."

"I think Tim should be the spokesman because they are his parents. How you talk to them is ex-

tremely important. What if you begin by saying something like this: 'Mom and Dad, I love you very much. I think you know that. Marie also loves you very much, and our children think you are wonderful grandparents. We want to continue to have a good relationship with you, and we want our children to enjoy you as grandparents. I know that your intentions are good, and you really love us as we love you. I want us to find a way to do this that will be good for all of us. I know that in the past you have told me that I don't need to call when I am coming by for a visit or to pick up something from Dad's shop. But I've always felt that I should respect your privacy by letting you know that I was coming. It seems to me that a phone call makes it easier for everybody. Sometimes when you show up at our house without calling, it is at a very inconvenient time. For example, last week when you came over at 8:00 on Tuesday night, we had put the children to bed early so that we could have a romantic time together. We were in the middle of lovemaking when the doorbell rang and you walked in. I think you can see how that was not the best time for a visit.'"

Marie interrupted and said to Tim, "Do you think you can say that to your parents?"

"I think so," Tim said. "In fact, that may be the one thing that may wake them up."

"Then, you can throw out some possibilities of what might be done to improve the situation, such as calling before they come and asking if it is a convenient time to come. If not, then suggest a time that would be convenient. A second idea would be to set a weekly time for them to visit. For example, Thursday night could be 'fun night with grandparents.' This will allow you to plan ahead and make it a fun evening for everyone. Of course, you could also periodically call and invite them to come over for dinner or to help you with a project you are working on. When you initiate the call, they have the choice to come or not to come. You have opened the door and let them know that you would like to have them. What you are trying to communicate to your parents is that you want them to be very involved in your lives and the lives of your children, but you want to do it in a manner that would be pleasant for everyone.

"I think if you take this approach, you may well find that your parents will be open. They may not fully understand why you would request this, but I think they would be willing to work with you. My guess is that their intention is not to make your lives miserable. They simply want to be involved in your lives and the lives of your children. It's just that the way they are doing it has become frustrating for you."

"And what if they don't pick up on these ideas and continue to show up whenever and wherever?" Marie asked.

"Then you will need to take the 'tough love' approach," I said. "At that point, you will need to make an appointment with me, and we will discuss how to show 'tough love' to in-laws who are not willing to respect your privacy. However, I really believe that if you take this approach, affirming them for their interest in your lives and expressing appreciation for all that they are doing for you, they are likely to respond to your request."

"Thanks," Tim said. "I really appreciate your taking time to talk with us."

"Let me know what happens," I said.

"We will," Marie said, "and I hope we don't have to make a visit to your office."

I nodded and reached for my Cheerios.

About six weeks later, I received a phone call from Tim. "I thought I should call and let you know how things have worked out," he said. "I had the talk with my folks shortly after we saw you in the grocery store. Dad was very understanding. Mom said she was hurt that it had come to this; she thought that family should be able to visit each other whenever they desired. I told her I understood her thoughts, but it just wasn't working for us. I think that after our conversation Dad must have talked to her, because a week later she seemed to be fine with the new arrangement. We established Thursday night as the night they would come for a visit. And so far, it seems to be working well. We did invite them over for dinner last Saturday night, and that also went well. I can sense a little tension with Mom, but I think she's coming around. I really appreciate your helping us with this because it was getting to be a real problem."

"I'm glad things are working out," I said. "When parents and their married children show respect for each other's privacy, it makes for healthy relationships. Let me know if I can ever help you in the future."

"Thanks," Tim said.

I have shared this illustration because the invasion of privacy is a common area of conflict with in-laws. Many couples wait until they are so frustrated with their in-laws that in a moment of intense anger, they lash out with harsh and condemning words and fracture the relationship. Sometimes these broken relationships stay fractured for years. But when the younger couple show respect for their parents' and in-laws' intentions and openly share with them their own frustrations, most of the problems can be resolved.

However, if in-laws insist they have a right to show up whenever and wherever, the couple will need to turn to the "tough love" approach, which may mean meeting the parents at the door and saying, "I'm sorry. But this is not a convenient time for you to visit. I'm in the midst of giving the children their baths, and then they must go to bed. I would love to have you visit, but right now is not a convenient time. If you like, I will call you tomorrow and suggest a time that would be convenient for all of us."

If the in-laws walk off in a huff, that is not your responsibility. You are doing what is best for your family and ultimately what is best for your relationship with your in-laws. If, in fact, you call the next day and suggest a time when they might come by, they have two options: They can accept your invitation, and if so, the pattern of intrusion on privacy will likely have been broken. Or they can say, "No, thank you. That is not a convenient time for us," in which case you might say, "I can understand that. Let me know when you would like to come and I will try to work it out." If they don't contact you for two or three weeks, don't panic. They are still trying to process their own feelings and thoughts. Give them time. If they don't call you, you can call them again in three weeks and give them another invitation. If they don't accept that invitation, perhaps you will want to wait until they initiate a call.

On your part, you keep the door open to have a relationship with them. If they choose to be obstinate and accuse you of pushing them out of your lives, you will know in your heart it is not true. You are simply trying to have a relationship built on respect of privacy.

SHOWING RESPECT FOR THEIR IDEAS

Jeremy's brother-in-law suggested that now was a good time to sell his house and buy a bigger one, not only because Jeremy and Peggy were expecting a baby but because "the interest rates have never been lower. It's a good time to sell your house and a good time to buy another." Jeremy had not thought about moving until his brother-in-law shared the idea. As he and Peggy reflected upon the idea, they both agreed that his brother-in-law was right. They immediately started the processes of looking for a house that would meet their needs and of putting their house on the market. That was five years ago. Jeremy has often said to Peggy, "I really appreciate your brother's encouraging us to move. This house is so much better for us than the one we had, and the payments are almost the same."

Whatever the topic of discussion, we all have different ideas. Our ideas are based upon our history, education, vocation, and social experience. Because no one human can know everything, we often turn to others for ideas in areas of life where we have had little experience. Such openness to the ideas of others is a sign of wisdom. The Scriptures indicate that when we seek the wise counsel of others, we are far more likely to make a wise decision.[4] The mature person is always looking for wisdom, even if it is spoken by a mother-in-law. When parents and in-laws make suggestions, their ideas should be given due consideration. After all, they are older and perhaps wiser than we are.

A good example of the wisdom of a father-in-law is found in Exodus 18. Moses was working from

morning to evening judging the people of Israel. The waiting room was always filled, and there was no time for coffee breaks. Moses' father-in-law said, "What you are doing is not good. You and these people who come to you will only wear yourselves out. The work is too heavy for you; you cannot handle it alone. Listen now to me and I will give you some advice."[5]

His father-in-law then suggested that the crowds be divided into thousands, hundreds, fifties, and tens and that authority be delegated to other qualified men who would judge those under their jurisdiction. Moses then would be free to spend more time with God and in teaching the people the law of God. Thus, his ministry would be more "preventive" than a "crisis" ministry. Only the difficult cases would be brought to him for judgment.[6]

Moses saw the wisdom of such a suggestion and adopted it. In so doing, he revealed his own maturity. He did not have to rebel against a good idea just because it came from his father-in-law. He was secure enough in his own self-worth that he could accept a good idea regardless of its source.

Respecting the ideas of your in-laws and giving those ideas reflective thought is a sign of maturity, not a sign of weakness. On the other hand, if you are the in-law who is making the suggestion or giving advice, let me encourage you to respect the freedom of those you are advising. Don't ever seek to force your ideas upon other persons. Ideas should be shared as suggestions, not as demands. If you are receiving advice from in-laws and feel they are seeking to control your decision, then it is your responsibility to listen carefully to the suggestion; give it your best consideration and then make the decision you believe best for you and your family. If your in-laws become upset that you did not follow their idea, you can express appreciation for their being willing to share their thoughts. Let them know that you did give consideration to the idea but that you made the decision you felt was best. Respecting their ideas does not mean that you will always follow their advice. After all, the responsibility for the decision rests upon your shoulders, not upon the shoulders of your in-laws.

SHOWING RESPECT FOR YOUR IN-LAWS' PECULIARITIES

Someone has said, "All of us are different but some of us are more different than others." When you begin to know your spouse's parents and siblings, you may encounter what to you are very weird behaviors. They may not be weird to your spouse because he or she has grown up with the behavior. For example, Pam found it very strange that her father-in-law spent every Saturday alone, away from the family. During hunting season, he was hunting. When he wasn't hunting, he was fishing or golfing. He saw Saturdays as his day of recreation, which he pronounced "re-creation." "It's my way of recuperating from the hard week of work," he said.

Pam felt this was unfair to his wife and children, but his wife and children seemed to accept it as normal. Pam asked her husband, Phil, "Did your father never take you fishing?"

"He did," Phil said, "but not on Saturdays."

"How about hunting?"

"A few times, but again, not on Saturday."

"How about golfing?" she asked.

"No. He said golfing was a man's sport, not for boys."

"Did you never want to go hunting, fishing, or golfing on Saturday with your father?" Pam inquired.

"I did, but Mom told me that was his day to relax, so I spent time playing with my brother and the boys in the neighborhood."

"Do you think your mother resented his time away every Saturday?"

"Perhaps at first," Phil said, "but I think she came to accept it. I never heard them argue about it."

"Well, you do know that I would never accept that in our relationship, right?"

"Yes," Phil said. "You don't have to worry. I want to spend time with you and the children on Saturday. I have no desire to isolate myself in recreation."

"Good," said Pam, "because if you were like your father, you and I would have a major battle."

Pam so much wanted to say to her father-in-law, "Do you know how foolish you have been over the years? Do you understand how self-centered you were? In my opinion, you were a poor model of a husband and father." However, she was wise enough to know that if she took that condemning approach, she would make herself an enemy. She also realized that it was not her place to tell her father-in-law how to live his life. She chose to accept that as a part of him that she did not understand. If her mother-in-law had been able to accept the Saturday recreational philosophy, then she would also accept it, even though in her mind it was a very strange practice.

Little things about your in-laws can be major irritants to you. Marcy was frustrated that her brother-in-law never opened the car door for her sister. Besides that, he wore a ball cap all the time, even inside the house. Her mother had taught her and her sister that ball caps were for ball games and that any gentleman should remove his hat when he walks in a house. She saw her brother-in-law as uncouth and disrespectful of her sister. She felt sad that her sister had married a man who was so inconsiderate.

When she talked with her sister about it, her sister said, "Yes. I would prefer that my husband open doors for me and that he take his ball cap off when he enters a home. But he is such a good man and treats me so well that I don't have the heart to make an issue of those things. In the big picture, they are rather small to me." Having voiced her opinion and heard her sister's response, Marcy decided to let it go. She still had her preferences, and if it were her husband, she would never accept those practices. But if it was fine with her sister, she would not wage a battle with her brother-in-law.

On a thousand fronts, we may be irritated with our in-laws. However, we must choose our battles carefully. Some things are not worth fighting over, and some things are clearly not our battles. Learning to respect the peculiarities of our in-laws is necessary if we are to have harmonious in-law relationships. In fact, if we were to fight our in-laws over every issue that strikes us as odd, we would spend the rest of our lives in battle.

In-laws were not designed to be enemies; they were designed to be friends. Showing respect for each others' holiday traditions, religious beliefs, privacy, ideas, and peculiarities is the road to friendship.

PUTTING THE PRINCIPLES INTO PRACTICE

What struggles do you face in the following areas?

1. Respecting holiday traditions

2. Respecting religious differences

3. Respecting privacy

4. Respecting the ideas of in-laws

5. Respecting your in-laws' peculiarities

Discuss with your spouse how you might improve in-law relationships by showing more respect.

3

The frustration in in-law relationships often becomes so intense that we find ourselves making condemning statements. We try to listen before we speak and to respect our in-laws, but things keep getting worse. So we lose control and launch an all-out attack. I remember Margot, who said, "I can't believe I called my daughter-in-law a whore. I guess I had just had it with her little flirty, suggestive behavior. She dresses like a prostitute so I called her one. I don't know if she will ever speak to me again, and my son is also upset with me."

Margot was following a pattern that is all too common in in-law relationships. We all have our perception of what is wrong with another person. We allow our hurt and resentment to grow, and then we attack with vicious words that we later regret. Many of these condemning words are characterized by speaking for the other person. That is, we have reached our conclusions as to the kind of person they are. We have determined what we think their behavior means, and we speak for them. "You are irresponsible and disrespectful."

What Margot said in the heat of anger was, "You little whore. You dress like a prostitute, and I'm surprised you haven't been raped. You are going to destroy your marriage. Why don't you think about the children?" Each "you" statement was like another exploding grenade further destroying their relationship. If Margot does not sincerely apologize, her daughter-in-law truly may never speak to her again.

When we begin a sentence with *you,* we are speaking as though we have ultimate knowledge of the situation. In reality, we are giving only a perception of you. Such statements come across as condemning and will likely stimulate a defensive response from your in-laws. We end up in a major argument, and both of us go away resenting the other.

There is a simple technique that will help you break this destructive pattern. It's called "speaking for yourself." It begins by learning to make "I" statements as opposed to "you" statements. For example, "I feel hurt," rather than "You hurt me." If you begin the sentence with "I," you are reporting or revealing your feelings. If you begin the sentence with "you," it is an attack. "You" statements are like verbal grenades, which bring hurt, resentment, and often counterattacks. "I" statements reveal a problem without condemning the other person.

Margot's daughter-in-law was not an immoral woman. While her idea of modest dress was quite different from her mother-in-law's, she was not intentionally trying to attract other men. Had Margot used "I" statements in conveying her concerns, the outcome might have been totally different. She might have said, "I'm fearful for your marriage. I feel like a lot of men interpret your behavior as an invitation. I don't think this is what you want. So, I'm not being critical of you; I'm just concerned. I want the best for you and Jerry." The daughter-in-law might still have been hurt or upset, but she would likely have worked through her feelings and understood Margot's concerns. When you speak for yourself, you are making valid statements. You are revealing *your* thoughts, feelings, desires, and perceptions. "I think . . ." "I feel . . ." "I wish . . ." "My perception is . . ." All these statements are valid because they are revealing what is going on inside *you*. You are speaking for yourself.

When you make "you" statements, you are always wrong because you never fully know what is going on inside another person. Even when you make positive "you" statements, you are speaking beyond your knowledge. "You are the most beautiful person in the world." This is certainly a positive statement but not a valid statement because you are speaking for all the people in the world. We know what you mean, and it will probably be accepted as a compliment. However, it would be more realistic to say, "I think that you are the most beautiful person I have ever seen." Now the statement seems sincere and not just flattery.

When you are expressing negative ideas, it is even more important to speak for yourself. Neal's mother, Betty, made unkind statements about his wife, Jan. She accused Jan of being lazy. "Why is she not working?" she asked Neal. "She should be helping you. Together, you could make enough money to buy a house and not have to waste money on rent." Betty continued her critical speech and concluded with, "Honey, I just want the best for you. I hate to see Jan wasting time."

Everything within Neal wanted to say, "You don't understand. You have no right to criticize Jan. You need to keep your mouth shut and stay out of our lives." Fortunately, Neal had had some training on how to speak for himself. So he began, "I'm glad you shared your thoughts with me. I did not know you were feeling that way. I can understand your concern, and I appreciate it. However, I need to share with you that Jan and I have talked about her working, and both of us have agreed that it would be best if she finished her college degree first. She is taking online classes and will finish next May. We both feel good about what we are doing, but thanks for sharing your concerns."

In speaking for himself, Neal averted an unnecessary battle with his mother. When your in-laws come at you with condemning statements, to counterattack is to start an unnecessary war. It is far better to respond with "I" statements that reveal your perspective in a positive manner.

The greatest hindrance to speaking for yourself is negative emotions. Hurt, anger, resentment, and fear push us to strike back. But striking back leads to arguments, and arguments lead to broken relationships. That is why I suggest that when you are attacked by your in-laws, take a deep and deliberate breath, followed by a moment of silence, before you speak. This may help you get on the "I" train rather than the "you" train.

Speaking for yourself is a learned pattern of speech. Most of us grew up getting "you" messages. "You disappointed me" and "You disobeyed me" were messages you heard from your parents. "You make me so angry," "You lied to me," and "You are irresponsible" are statements your parents may have made to each other.

How do you break out of this destructive, condemning pattern? By conscious choice. First, you must recognize the value of speaking for yourself; then you must try it. Perhaps it would help if you stood in front of the mirror and said, "I feel hurt," "I feel angry," "I feel disappointed," "I feel like you deceived me," or "I feel like you do not trust me." When you practice making "I" statements, you are more likely to make them in the context of live conversations.

You will not establish the art of speaking for yourself overnight. From time to time, you will hear yourself begin a sentence with "you." When you start a sentence with "You are doing . . .," catch yourself and say instead, "Let me say that again. I feel that what you are doing . . ." When you restate your sentence with "I" instead of "you," you are not only learning to speak for yourself but also modeling the process to your in-laws.

In time, you can learn to speak for yourself. When you do, you will have learned an important skill in becoming friends with your in-laws.

PUTTING THE PRINCIPLES INTO PRACTICE

1. Listen to yourself talk. How many of your sentences begin with "You . . . ," especially when you are upset? "You" statements start arguments.

2. The next time you have negative feelings, stand in front of a mirror and practice saying, "I feel hurt," "I feel angry," "I feel disappointed," or "I feel like you deceived me." Then, use the appropriate "I" statement when you talk to the person at whom you are angry.

3. When you start your sentence with "You make me . . . ," catch yourself and say instead, "Let me say that differently. I feel hurt when you say that."

4

SEEK TO NEGOTIATE

"*W*hy can't we go see Grandmother?" a seven-year-old asks.

Her mother replies, "Because Grandmother doesn't want to see us right now."

"Why?" asks the child.

"Because the last time we were there, your brother marked with crayons on Grandmother's wall. She wants to wait until you and your brother get older before we go back to her house."

"I won't mark on her walls."

"I know that, honey, but Grandmother doesn't know that. It cost her lots of money to put up new wallpaper, and she is upset right now."

"When will she stop being upset?"

"I don't know. Right now we are trying to work that out."

"We're trying to work that out." That is what negotiation is all about. To negotiate is to discuss an issue in order to reach an agreement. Negotiation is the opposite of withdrawal and resentment. When we negotiate, we are choosing to believe that there is an answer, and with God's help, we will find it.

Why is negotiation so important? Because without negotiation, fractured relationships may continue for years. Imagine the tragedy if, at age twelve, the girl mentioned above is still asking, "Why can't we go see Grandmother?" When we do not negotiate our differences, we allow walls to stand between us and our in-laws, and the potential for becoming friends with our in-laws evaporates.

Anger is often the enemy of negotiation. Perhaps as you read the illustration above, your thoughts were, "If that's the way the grandmother feels, then forget it. I would never take my kids back to see her. If her walls are more important to her than my children, then I wouldn't care if we had a relationship." Even though these thoughts are understandable if followed, they would sabotage negotiation and leave you with broken in-law relationships for a lifetime. Everyone loses when we allow anger to push us into an unyielding stance of opposition.

Healthy in-law relationships require negotiation for one simple reason: We are all humans. Humans think differently and experience different emotions and reactions. Without negotiation, we allow our differences to become divisive. I have experienced some of my deepest pain in the counseling office as I have listened to the stories of in-laws who haven't spoken to each other for years because someone refused to negotiate. For the sake of your spouse and your children, I urge you to abandon your stubbornness and learn the art of negotiating.

We have just looked at three essential skills that prepare you to negotiate. First, we discussed the necessity of listening before you speak. Ask questions with a view to understanding the thoughts and feelings of your in-laws. Second, show respect for their ideas. You may not agree with their ideas but you give them the freedom to be human, which means they have a perspective different from your own. Third, speak for yourself. Make "I" statements, not "you" statements. With those skills in mind, I want to share some steps in the process of negotiating:

MAKE PROPOSALS

Negotiation begins with someone making a proposal; someone must break the silence. Silence indicates that something is wrong. Someone did or said something that offended an in-law. Perhaps we exchanged a few harsh words and then withdrew in silence. Or perhaps we went immediately to the silent mode, saying nothing aloud but talking to ourselves and wallowing in hurt and anger. While momentary silence can be a positive response to anger, silence must never become a lifestyle. Give yourself time to cool down emotionally. Then it's time to make a proposal. Hopefully, the silence endured only for a day or two at most. The longer a silence endures, the more difficult it is to break. But breaking the silence is a necessity if we are going to improve in-law relationships.

Martha, the mother of the son who had marked on his grandmother's walls, called her mother-in-law and said, "I feel really bad about Jason marking on your walls. If I had the money, I would pay to have them repaired. I don't have the money, and that makes me feel even worse. I do want my children to have a good relationship with you, so I'm wondering if you could meet us at the park Thursday afternoon at two. They both really want to see you. Would that possibly fit into your schedule?" With this proposal, Martha has apologized for her son's behavior and has expressed her regret and her desire to make things right. She has also offered an opportunity for the grandmother to be with the grandchildren in a setting that has no potential for bringing harm to her house. If the grandmother responds positively, then the relationship is on the mend.

Proposals should be realistic and take into account the offense that was committed. This normally means that we begin with an apology, accepting our responsibility and being willing to make restitution when possible. The apology is then followed with a proposal that offers an opportunity for the relationship to continue. You may still feel hurt, and you may not fully understand why your in-law was so offended, but you are choosing to seek negotiation rather than withdrawing in resentment. Your proposal opens the opportunity for the two of you to take steps in a positive direction.

Good proposals are specific, as opposed to general. Rather than saying, "The children really miss you, and I do hope that we can get together soon," Martha made a proposal for a specific day, time, and place. General proposals are too nebulous to be helpful. Had Martha given a general proposal, it might have been several weeks or months before her mother-in-law responded. When she made her proposal specific, she made it easy for her mother-in-law to respond. And the process of reconciliation could begin much sooner.

John and Kim were in my office complaining that John's father had given their two children chewing gum, even after they had asked him not to. They were toying with the idea of not allowing the children to stay with their grandparents because they didn't trust John's father.

Being a grandfather myself, I was smiling on the inside, but I knew that John and Kim were serious. To them, it was not just a matter of chewing gum. It was a matter of trust. They felt that if they could not trust John's father to follow their expressed rules, then maybe it was better to keep the children away from him.

I listened to them carefully, asked clarifying questions, and then said to them, "I think I understand your concern. I'm sure that if I were in your shoes, I would feel the same way. Now let me share my thoughts." (How's that for being a good listener?)

I acknowledged that John and Kim were certainly free to keep their children away from his father, but in my opinion, negotiation was better than withdrawal. Withdrawal removes the opportunity for the relationship to improve, whereas negotiation opens the door to the possibility of a better relationship.

I suggested that they make a positive proposal to John's father. That proposal would involve expressing to him how disappointed they were that he had not honored their rules. They would also explain why they had made the rule of no chewing gum. (It had come as a recommendation from their dentist.) John and Kim knew that John's father was a Monopoly player. So they would say to John's father, "We know the children love you and you love them, and we want you to have a good relationship with them. Therefore, we are going to give you a 'Get out of jail free card' for this offense. But the next time you give them chewing gum, you will 'Go directly to jail,' you will not 'Proceed past Go' and you will not 'Receive $200.' Do you understand?"

I encouraged them to do all this with a smile. They agreed that if John's father received their proposal in a positive way, they would continue visits as normal. However, if John's father went into an angry rage and told them that they were not going to tell him what to do with his own grandchildren and that he would give them chewing gum whenever he pleased, they would say to John's father, "If that's your decision, then we will have to keep the children away from you. If you ever change your mind, we will allow them to spend time with you."

We all knew that if this situation developed, John's mother would work on John's father and within a few weeks, he would decide not to give the children chewing gum. At that point, they could then make another proposal or his father might even call with a proposal himself.

If John's father had taken this belligerent attitude, he would have been indicating that he was not open to negotiation. In cases like this, we must withdraw for a season before making another proposal. But maybe John's father would come back and say, "Can we make two exceptions? I could give them chewing gum on their birthdays, and secondly, I could give them a cookie instead of chewing gum from time to time." That would demonstrate an openness to negotiate, which would then give

John and Kim the chance to say, "We are open to chewing gum once a year on the children's birthdays. Cookies should be given only as dessert, not between meals."

John's father can accept their counterproposal or offer another proposal, and together they come to an agreement. That is the purpose of negotiating, and it brings us to the second step in the process.

BE OPEN TO SOMETHING DIFFERENT

Making a proposal is the first step in the process of negotiating. The second step is listening carefully to counterproposals. Remember, negotiating has to do with two people trying to understand each other and reach an agreement that both of them will feel good about. Because we are different, we have different ideas. A proposal opens the opportunity for dialogue. I listen carefully to your proposal. Then I bring my own thoughts and feelings to play and suggest perhaps a major or minor change to what you are suggesting. Then you have an opportunity to hear my counterproposal and perhaps make a counterproposal of your own. The process of listening, understanding, and seeking to find an agreement is the process of negotiation.

People who learn to negotiate well are people who learn to respect the ideas of others, even when they disagree. We listen because we respect them as individuals and want to understand their thoughts and feelings. If you don't fully understand their proposal, by all means ask clarifying questions.

For example, John's father might have asked, "Are you saying that you don't want the children to have chewing gum because you think the sugar is bad for them?" to which John or Kim would have replied, "Our concern is for their teeth. Our dentist advised against letting the children have chewing gum because their teeth are in a very crucial stage of development, and he felt that it would be detrimental for them to chew gum at this time." Had the father been willing to ask clarifying questions, he would have understood the situation more clearly.

When we make a proposal, we should expect a counterproposal. We must not come to negotiation with the attitude "It's my way or no way at all." We come with the attitude "Here's an idea that I think will work. What do you think about it?" We are open to hear their thoughts and open to their ideas. It is this openness to alternative ideas that gives us the ability to reach agreements.

When we are rigid in our ideas and unwilling to consider an alternative, we stymie the process of negotiation. Keep in mind that there are reasons behind your in-laws' counterproposal. If it doesn't seem logical to you, continue to ask questions of them so that they can clarify why they think their idea is workable.

Negotiation is a process of proposals and counterproposals, where all parties are seeking to find an agreement. If you are willing to continue the process of negotiation, you will likely find an agreement.

LOOK FOR A WIN-WIN SOLUTION

The third step in the process of negotiating is finding a solution that both parties feel is workable. It may not be what either one of you desired at the beginning of the negotiation, but it will be a solution that addresses your key concerns. Both of you come away from the agreement feeling that you have taken a positive step in developing your relationship. This is what I like about negotiating. We end up moving in a positive direction and moving together. This is good for in-law relationships.

Betsy and Bill were at odds with Betsy's mother, Joyce. Joyce had informed them that she was taking their children to the beach for a vacation the second week in June. She was telling them in January so they would have plenty of notice. The problem was that Bill and Betsy had already enrolled the children for children's camp at their church that same week.

Joyce was shocked and angry that they had made that decision without talking with her. "I told you I wanted to take the children on a vacation to the beach this summer. Why didn't you discuss it with me before you signed them up for camp?" she asked.

Betsy responded, "Mom, there's only one week for children's camp; they either go that week or they don't go at all. We really wanted them to go to camp this year. We assumed that you could take them to the beach any week during the summer."

"Well, I could, but I have already rented this place at the beach, and I don't know if I can get my money back."

"Then maybe you should have talked with us before you rented the place," Betsy said. "It sounds like we both could have done a little better job at communicating with each other."

Both parties had good intentions. They each wanted to do something worthwhile for the children. The crisis developed because of lack of communication.

Situations like this arise regularly in in-law relationships. These situations call for negotiation. Someone needs to make a proposal and get the process started. In this case, Betsy's mother made the first proposal: "What if I check with the rental company to see if I can rent the same facility a different week?"

"That sounds like a good place to start," Betsy said. "We certainly would like for the children to have a week with you at the beach. I know they would enjoy it."

Three days later Betsy's mother came back with this report: "They will allow me to rent the facility for a different week, but it will be a seventy-five-dollar change fee. I tried to talk them out of it, but they say it's their policy. I hate to waste money like that. Have you checked with your church to make sure that the children's camp is that week? They are not likely to change the dates between now and then, are they?"

"I did check," Betsy said, "and they have the facility rented. It's the week they do children's camp every summer, and it's not going to change." Then Betsy made a proposal. "What if Bill and I pay the seventy-five-dollar change fee for you? It would be a small investment for us to have the children with you for a whole week at the beach. We wouldn't mind doing that. I know you are already paying an arm and a leg to rent the place for the week. That's the least we can do."

Betsy's mother replied, "I hate for you to do that. It's just a waste of money."

"I don't see it as wasting money, Mom. I see it as the cost of our not talking to each other before we made decisions. So, let's just look at it as a seventy-five-dollar learning experience on our part. I think we have both learned the importance of communication before we make commitments." Joyce agreed and the problem was solved. They both went away feeling good about the decision.

When both of us walk away as winners, we know that the negotiation has been successful. When one of us is walking away with resentment, it is a sign that we need further negotiation. Our objective should always be to reach an agreement that makes both of us winners.

Notice that I entitled this chapter "Seek to Negotiate." I would be less than honest if I did not admit that there are some in-laws who will not negotiate. These people have rigid personalities. If you do not agree with them, then you have a problem.

However, even with these individuals, I would still encourage you to seek to negotiate. Make a proposal. Who knows? Maybe they will agree with your proposal. And if so, the problem is solved. On the other hand, perhaps they will be unwilling to budge.

If you can accept their position, fine. If not, you have to make a decision. Will you simply withdraw and acknowledge that the relationship is fractured? Or will you accept something with which you disagree in order to keep the peace? You will have to decide whether or not the issue is big enough to fracture the relationship. Some things we can live with even though we don't like them. Other things are too major for us to accept. Not all in-law relationships can be healed, but it is always worth the effort to seek negotiation.

PUTTING THE PRINCIPLES INTO PRACTICE

1. Is there an in-law to whom you need to make a proposal? If so, why not break the silence and share your proposal? Take the first step in negotiation.

2. Has an in-law made a proposal to you? Can you accept it, or do you need to make a counterproposal?

3. Are you willing to listen to the ideas of your in-laws, or do you have the attitude, "It's my way or no way at all"?

4. To negotiate is to discuss an issue in order to reach an agreement. Ask God to help you learn the art of negotiation.

5

MAKE REQUESTS, NOT DEMANDS

*I*n the last few years, we have been hearing more and more about "grandparents' rights." I remember one grandmother who said to me, "Our daughter will not let us see our grandchildren. We are thinking about suing her. It's just not right that they would keep the grandchildren away from us."

"What reasons do they give?" I inquired.

"They say it's because we keep beer and liquor in the house. My husband, George, is an alcoholic, and they say they don't want their children to grow up to be alcoholics. But that's absurd. George has been an alcoholic for twenty years. I don't drink alcohol at all, and I've lived with him all these years. Being around an alcoholic does not make one an alcoholic."

"How long have they been keeping the children away from you?" I asked.

"Since last Christmas," she said. "About nine months now."

"Did something happen last Christmas that influenced their decision?" I asked.

"Well, one evening, George had too much to drink. He was in a jovial mood. He poured a little beer in glasses and told the children, 'Let's make a toast to Santa Claus.' The kids went along with him, drank the beer, and then started gagging. My daughter and son-in-law rushed into the kitchen to find out what was going on. When they realized what he had done, they immediately took the children home and told us they would never return again. My husband cursed them as they left the house and told them how stupid they were. I know that what George did was wrong, but what they are doing is also wrong. Grandparents have rights too. I have told them that I would personally take all the alcohol out of the house and store it in the garage and would promise them that my husband would not drink while they were here. But that's not enough for them. I don't know what else to do; that's why I'm thinking about suing them."

"You could do that," I said, "but what if you win the suit and your daughter and son-in-law are forced to let you see the children under supervised conditions? How satisfactory would that be?"

"I know what you're saying," she said. "That's not really what I want. I just want to have a good relationship with my daughter, our son-in-law, and our grandchildren. And I don't know what to do."

"How severe is your husband's drinking problem?" I asked.

"He has been in and out of treatment programs for twenty years," she said. "He'll do fine for a while, but once he falls off the wagon, he may go on a drinking binge for a month. He's had a hard time keeping jobs. It's been really hard to live with him, but I love him and keep hoping that things will get better. I know he feels bad about not seeing the grandchildren too. We've talked about it."

As a counselor, I was deeply moved by the pain I saw in her face. I said, "Sometimes when alcoholics realize they are losing something really valuable to them, they are highly motivated to stop drinking. Do you think George would be willing to talk with me about it?"

"He might, if he thought it would help the situation," she said.

"Then tell him that I would very much like to see him, that I have some ideas I think may be helpful."

Over the next few weeks, I was able to get her husband enrolled in a Christian treatment program. I assured him that God would give him the power to conquer alcohol and that I believed this was a major step in restoring a relationship with his daughter, son-in-law, and grandchildren. After the initial treatment program and while he was actively involved in a Christian support group, I began to talk with George about the power of apologizing to his daughter and son-in-law for his behavior last Christmas.

I told him apologies are only meaningful when they are sincere expressions of regret over our behavior. "An apology is accepting responsibility for your behavior, acknowledging that it was wrong, and requesting forgiveness. An apology is not a demand for forgiveness," I said. "It is a request for forgiveness. Your daughter and son-in-law may not be ready to forgive you, but your request will be the first step."

Together we crafted a carefully worded apology with which he felt comfortable. I asked if he would give me permission to call his daughter and son-in-law and invite them to my office so we could talk with them together about what was going on in his life. He agreed, and they accepted my invitation.

In that meeting, I shared with the young couple my involvement with the wife's father in trying to help him deal with his alcohol problem. I told them that I knew he had tried to quit drinking many times through the years but I believed that this time he had truly put his trust in God and he was going to be successful. Then I gave George an opportunity to talk.

I listened as he not only shared the apology we had written but, with tears, poured out his heart. He apologized for his past failures to his daughter when she was growing up, acknowledging that he knew that he had embarrassed her many times while she was in high school, that he had failed to be the father she deserved, and that he knew that what he had done last Christmas was the most painful thing he had ever done to her. He told her how many times he had relived that scene in his mind and how bad he felt about it.

"I know I don't deserve forgiveness," he said, "but I'm asking for it. I'm not asking you to let me see the children, though I would very much like to apologize to them. I'm looking forward to my first sober Christmas in twenty years. I know that you may not be there, though I wish you would be. I would like an opportunity to make the future different. And I would like to be the kind of father that you can trust. I love you very much, and I am so sorry for what I've done to hurt you."

His daughter showed no signs of emotion. I assumed that she had heard apologies in the past but had never seen changed behavior. My guess was she questioned whether this was sincere and whether things would be different in the future.

Eventually, she said to him, "Dad, I want to forgive you. But it may take some time. I've been hurt so badly. I want to believe that what you are saying is true, and I guess the next few months will show me. I hope you understand that as much as I want to forgive you, it will take me a little time."

"I understand," her father said. "I appreciate your meeting with us today because I so much wanted to apologize to you."

The conversation ended. I offered my services to the young couple if they should ever want to talk with me further. And I told George that I would see him next week.

I never saw the young couple again, but George and his wife informed me that within a month their daughter had given her father an opportunity to apologize to the children and that the children had freely expressed forgiveness to him. After seeing the children's response, the daughter also expressed forgiveness to George. When Christmas rolled around, the daughter had given no indication that they would bring the children. But a week before Christmas, the children asked her if they could go see their grandparents at Christmas and the mother agreed.

At first, it was a little strained since the children had not been in their grandparents' home for a year. But before the evening was over, laughter again filled the house.

As the children were leaving, George said, "I just want to thank everybody for being here. This has been the best Christmas of my life. It's been a hard year for all of us, but it has been a year of tremendous change in my life. I want to be the kind of grandfather you children deserve. And I hope you will pray for me every day because I pray for you."

When George and his wife shared the Christmas story with me, I knew that evening marked the beginning of a new quality of relationship. And the timing reminded me that the healing of relationships is what Christmas is all about.

I share this story because it illustrates that positive in-law relationships are not built upon demands, but upon requests. Had the grandparents tried to demand their "rights" by legally forcing their daughter and son-in-law to let them see the grandchildren, it would likely have led to a lifetime of estrangement. But because they were willing to humble themselves, acknowledge their part in the broken relationship, follow the road of genuine change, honestly deal with the problem, and then request forgiveness, they found the healing desired. Good in-law relationships cannot be built on the principle of demanding our rights. The Scriptures say "[Love] does not demand its own way."[1]

This principle is illustrated in the life of Jesus. On one occasion, after Jesus had been teaching some rather difficult things, the Scriptures tell us, "At this point many of his disciples turned away and deserted him. Then Jesus turned to the Twelve and asked, 'Are you also going to leave?' Simon Peter replied, 'Lord, to whom would we go? You have the words that give eternal life. We believe, and we know you are the Holy One of God.'"[2]

Clearly Jesus was not demanding that the twelve disciples continue to walk with him. He had invited them in the beginning to follow him. Now on this occasion, he gave them the freedom to walk away. In fact, we know that one of the twelve did eventually walk away. But at this time, Peter spoke for the others when he said, "You have the words that give eternal life." They followed Jesus because they were convinced that he was "the Holy One of God."

In-law relationships must follow this model. We cannot force our in-laws to do what we believe to be "the right thing." We can and should make requests of them. If we have desires, these desires should be verbalized. If you wish your in-laws would visit more often, invite them to come more often. If you wish that they would come less often, then request that they come only on those occasions when you have time to spend with them. We must never expect our in-laws to read our minds. Making requests is a part of any good relationship.

Jesus taught that this principle of "making requests" applies also in our relationship with God. He said, "Keep on asking, and you will receive what you ask for . . . for everyone who asks, receives." Then he moved to the human plane. "You parents—if your children ask for a loaf of bread, do you give them a stone instead? Or if they ask for a fish, do you give them a snake? Of course not! So if you sinful people know how to give good gifts to your children, how much more will your heavenly Father give good gifts to those who ask him."[3]

Does this mean that God always gives us exactly what we ask? The obvious answer is *no*. He loves us too much to give us things that he knows will be detrimental to our well-being. But as our heavenly Father, he freely gives us good gifts in response to our requests.

Will your in-laws always respond to your request in exactly the way you desire? Probably not.

Nor will their response always be based on love. All of us have a tendency to be self-centered. Many times we respond to others' requests in a very self-ish way. However, making requests of in-laws is an important part of building positive relationships.

Ben, who was a novice fisherman, asked his father-in-law if he could borrow certain fishing gear. His father-in-law replied, "I can't let you borrow that one, but I'd be happy to loan you this one." Ben didn't know the difference between the two; his father-in-law did, and he didn't want to run the risk of losing a $600 piece of gear to an inexperienced fisherman.

Had Ben become angry with his father-in-law because he would not loan exactly what he had requested, their relationship would have been fractured. Instead, he gladly accepted his father-in-law's offer and had a good day fishing. People are responsible for their possessions. They choose to lend or not to lend, to give or not to give. The wise in-law will not get upset when a particular request is denied but will be grateful when a request is granted or a substitute offer is made.

It is often in making requests that in-law relationships are strengthened. Brittany asked her mother-in-law, Margie, if she would teach her to knit. Margie's response was, "I can't imagine that a girl of your generation would like to learn to knit. But if you would, then I would be happy to teach you."

Brittany assured her that she was sincere. Over the next several months, not only did Brittany learn to knit, but she and her mother-in-law developed a close relationship as a unique skill was passed from one generation to the next. When they took tea breaks, Brittany learned much about her mother-in-law, including the fact that it was Margie's own mother-in-law who had taught her to knit. Without knowing it, Brittany was continuing a family tradition.

In time Margie, who was a gregarious, always-happy kind of person, shared with Brittany some of her health struggles through the years. Later, when Margie was diagnosed with breast cancer, it was Brittany with whom she shared the news first. And it was Brittany who was her greatest emotional support through the months of chemotherapy and recovery. And it all began with a request: "Would you teach me how to knit?"

The Scriptures say, "It is more blessed to give than to receive."[4] When you make a request of your in-laws, you are giving them an opportunity. In responding to your request, they find greater happiness than you find in receiving what you have requested.

Requesting and giving are a part of the normal cycle of good relationships. From time to time all of us need or desire certain things that another has the capacity to fulfill. If we share these desires in the form of a request and the other person chooses to respond positively, we are forging a relationship that will be strong through the years. Conversely, when we make demands upon our in-laws, telling them what they should do and making them feel guilty when they don't do what we are demanding, we destroy a relationship. Good relationships are fostered by requesting and giving, not by demanding.

PUTTING THE PRINCIPLES INTO PRACTICE

1. What demands have your in-laws made of you? How did you respond?

2. What demands have you made of your in-laws? How did they respond?

3. What requests would you like to make of your in-laws? Consider making your request after expressing appreciation to your in-laws for something you admire about them.

4. What requests have your in-laws made of you? Consider responding with love to a request your in-laws have made.

6

GRANT THE GIFT OF FREEDOM

$\mathcal{T}$he greatest gift that parents can give their married children is the gift of freedom. In the introduction to this book, we talked about the biblical challenge for young couples to leave parents and establish a new family unit. Parents can make this easy or difficult. They can give the couple the freedom to leave, or they can continue to interject themselves into the young couple's lives and make independence extremely difficult.

Two types of individuals will have difficulty granting the gift of freedom. First are the people with a controlling personality. These are the people who think clearly, reach conclusions quickly, and assume that their ideas are always right. They are typically well-meaning people, but they are over-bearing, imposing their will on anyone who will allow it. They do not see themselves as controllers. They often genuinely feel that they are looking out for the best interest of the other person. This personality type will have great difficulty releasing their children to marriage. Their tendency will be to continue to impose their ideas on their married children and the son-in-law or daughter-in-law.

There is a second type of individual who will have trouble letting go. These are the people whose self-worth is tied up in the success of their chil-dren. They have done everything in their power to help their children succeed. They have put them in the best schools, provided for every financial need, and given loads of verbal encouragement. With ev-ery educational or vocational accomplishment of the child, the mother and father feel better about themselves. This pattern will not likely change when the child gets married. They will continue to reach out, doing everything they can to help the young couple succeed. The problem is that their "help" often comes across as "intrusion" and makes it more difficult for the young couple to establish their identity. Parental efforts to help often create arguments in the marriage and, thus, are detrimental to marital unity.

Kelly and Andy were in my office expressing frustration with Kelly's mother. Andy said, "She totally decorated our apartment. She chose the colors, she chose the fabrics, and she did everything. I feel like I'm living in someone else's house. It's nice, but it's not us. I would rather have no window treatments and wait until we can afford them. She felt like we needed to have everything now. I don't like her controlling our lives."

I looked at Kelly and asked, "How do you feel about all of this?"

"I really feel that it is my mother's way of showing us that she loves us. I don't think she wants to create a problem for us. I like the way she decorated our apartment. I would like to simply accept it as a gift, but Andy doesn't see it that way. That's why we're here. We feel like this is tearing us apart. If my mother knew that we were arguing about what she had done for us, she would be devastated."

I share this story because this illustrates several principles about controlling personalities. First, controllers seldom see themselves as controllers. They see themselves simply doing what is good or right. They have great difficulty understanding how others see them as controllers. Second, a controller typically marries someone with a compliant personality. If he or she had married a person with a controlling personality, life would be one huge battlefield. The compliant person is willing to accept most of what the controller does, although eventually it often becomes a source of irritation in the marriage.

My guess was that Andy himself had a controlling personality. He wanted to be in charge of determining how their apartment was decorated, and he wanted to pay for it. He saw this as his responsibility, and he wanted the freedom to do it. He found his mother-in-law's actions as an intrusion into their marriage.

Kelly, on the other hand, had a compliant personality. Through the years, she had learned to accept her mother's acts of control as gifts of love, which indeed they were. She had no need to be a part of the decision-making process; she was perfectly happy letting her mother make decisions for her. In fact, this made her life easier. It worked fine when she lived with only one controller—her mother. However, now she is married to another controller. Life becomes extremely difficult when two people are trying to tell you what to do.

To the mothers-in-law and fathers-in-law who are reading this book, I urge you to learn the art of backing off. Your married children deserve the freedom to make their own decisions. I know that your efforts to help them are done in good faith. You are genuinely expressing love and trying to help them have a better life.

However, your good intentions may be making life difficult for your sons or daughters. They may be willing to receive your help, as they have done through the years. However, their spouses may be unwilling, not because they are contrary but simply because they are human and have their own personality. People with similar personalities seldom marry each other. It is highly unlikely that a compliant child will marry a compliant spouse.

So what are in-laws to do when they genuinely want to help their married children? You share your idea and ask if they would find this helpful. (Make a request, not a demand.) Assure them that if they do not see it as helpful, you will certainly understand. Then give them time to discuss the issue and get back with you with their answer. If they accept your offer, you may proceed. If not, you must put your idea aside, granting them the gift of freedom.

The gift of freedom is a far more valuable gift than the gift of decorating an apartment. If you do not allow the couple the freedom to make their own decisions, insisting on doing things for them that you think will be helpful, you are in the process of creating resentment in the heart of your daughter-in-law or son-in-law. And you are stimulating unnecessary arguments between your child and his/her spouse.

Here are some additional ideas for mothers-in-law and fathers-in-law who sincerely desire to help their married children:

DON'T MAKE THE COUPLE DEPENDENT ON YOU

Marriage is about independence, not dependence. For the first twenty or so years of life, your children were dependent on you. Through high school and perhaps college and graduate school, you made it possible for them to reach their educational objectives. However, with marriage comes a paradigm shift. No longer is an adult, married child to be dependent upon you. The couple are to establish their own place in the world, learn to work together as a team to meet their own needs. You must encourage this independence, not lessen it.

Let me give you a negative and a positive example. Bill and Alice were a fairly successful middle-class couple. They made sure that their son Ken got a college education. When Ken got married shortly after college, they realized that his entry-level job would not allow him to buy a house anytime soon.

They adamantly objected to the concept of renting. They saw it as throwing money away. Therefore, they offered to make a down payment on a house and to give Ken and his new bride $500 a month toward their monthly mortgage payment. They were fully capable of doing this, and Ken and April were happy to receive it. They were thrilled to be in a house when most of their friends were living in apartments.

However, five years later, Bill died suddenly from a massive heart attack. It rocked the world of both families. When everything was settled, Alice had enough income to meet her own needs, but not enough to continue the $500 a month supplement to Ken and April.

Within two months, Ken and April were in a financial crisis. Ken's salary alone did not meet their monthly obligations. By this time, they had two small children. April really did not want to work outside the home, and Ken agreed. But they were faced with the choice of moving out of their house to something smaller or of April taking on at least a part-time job. April did in fact get a job but had a growing resentment toward Ken that she had to leave the children with a babysitter.

In retrospect, everyone realized that Bill and Alice—while sincerely trying to be helpful—had in fact created a major problem for Ken and his family. Ken and April said to me, "We wish we had started in an apartment like our friends and lived with less. I think we both would have been happier, and certainly we would not be under the stress we are now experiencing."

On the positive side, Sam and Audrey are examples of parents who discovered a way to give without making their children dependent upon their gifts. Their daughter Julie got married to Mike at the end of her junior year of college. Mike was also a rising senior. Sam and Audrey agreed to pay for Julie's final year in college, and Mike's parents did the same. After graduation, Mike started his own business, and Julie took an entry-level job with a local bank.

Mike knew he would not make much money in the first few years of his business, but they were both willing to sacrifice while Mike was getting the business off the ground. They lived in a very small apartment in a less than desirable neighborhood. They drove the old cars their parents had given them when they entered college. They bought furniture from Goodwill and lived very meagerly.

Whenever Sam and Audrey would visit with Mike and Julie, they would go home and talk about their desire to get them out of that apartment and into a respectable neighborhood. They knew that financially they had the ability to do it. On one occasion, they broached the idea with Mike and Julie and found both of them resistant to the idea of their help. Julie said, "Mother, we want to have a story to tell like you and Daddy. Remember the first place you lived after you were married? I have always admired you and your willingness to sacrifice while Dad was in the military and later when he came home to get his own business started. We know you love us and want to help us, but we would rather do it ourselves."

Audrey and Sam took Julie seriously and expressed their admiration and appreciation for her spirit. Never again did they bring up the subject. They gave the gift of freedom, and they have not regretted their choice. Today Mike's business is flourishing, and he and Julie have a nice house and a story to tell their children.

Please do not think I'm saying that you should never give gifts to your married children or help them financially. What I am saying is don't give your gift in such a way that it makes your adult children dependent on you to maintain their lifestyle. If their refrigerator goes out and you want to buy them a refrigerator, then ask if they would find this helpful and would appreciate your doing it. If they agree, then buy the refrigerator. It would be a one-time gift that meets an unexpected need and will be seen as an act of love. Your children will accept it with deep appreciation. On the other hand, I would not encourage you to agree to make the monthly loan payments if they buy a new car. Such payments normally last for a minimum of three years, and for those three years, they would be financially dependent upon your monthly help. This does not establish a pattern of independence.

DON'T GIVE GIFTS THAT AREN'T DESIRED

Alan and Betsy were boat enthusiasts. When they were a young couple, they bought their first boat. Throughout the lives of their children, they had enjoyed going to the lake almost every Saturday. When their daughter Angie married Rod, they expected that Rod and Angie would regularly meet them at the lake as they had often done when they were dating. However, after marriage, Rod got a job that required him to work most Saturdays. Angie became involved in an inner-city ministry with her church. So their pattern of joining her family at the lake was broken. Her parents missed this "family time" greatly and prayed for the day that Rod would get a different job.

After about a year, Rod did in fact get a new job that did not require Saturday work. Within a week, Alan and Betsy bought a boat for Rod and Angie, invited them to the lake, and revealed their surprise gift. Rod and Angie acted excited, but when they returned home, they both agreed that the last thing they ever wanted was a boat. Rod did not enjoy water sports, and Julie had developed a sincere interest in the ministry in which she was involved on Saturdays. Neither of them wanted to spend Sundays at the lake; they much preferred to be active in their church.

When Rod and Angie's boat stayed in storage weekend after weekend, Alan and Betsy realized that they had made a mistake. They thought that the boat would lure Rod and Angie to the lake and that they could have family times like they had before. But that was not happening.

Now they faced a parental choice. They could resent Rod and Angie for not being grateful for their gift and spending time with them at the lake. Or, they could admit that buying the boat without talking with Rod and Angie about it was a mistake and perhaps even an effort to manipulate them to come to the lake. They chose to accept responsibility for their well-intended but unwise choice in buying the boat. Other than the boat issue, Alan and Betsy had a good relationship with Rod and Angie. They often had dinner together, during which the relationship was always cordial and positive.

GARY CHAPMAN

Alan and Betsy wanted to keep this positive relationship, so they discussed a strategy to handle the boat. They agreed that if Rod and Angie were willing, they would sell the boat and give the money to Angie to use in her inner-city ministry. When they shared their idea with Rod and Angie, the young couple was elated.

Angie said, "Dad, I didn't want to tell you that we really didn't want the boat. I knew that it would hurt your feelings because I knew you bought it because you love us. But really, neither one of us is into boating. I enjoyed it as a child, but I am in a different stage of life now. I love what I'm doing on Saturdays with the kids. I can't tell you how proud I am of you for expressing this interest in what I'm doing. There are so many things that need to be done, and now, with this money, we will be able to do them. I love you so much and I appreciate your understanding." Rod affirmed Angie's comments, and the boat issue was settled.

Often our ideas of an appropriate gift will not seem appropriate to our adult children. Therefore, don't waste money on gifts that they will not appreciate. Ask before you give.

AFFIRM THE INTERESTS OF YOUR MARRIED CHILDREN

Throughout life, all of us develop interests in various pursuits. These may include educational, vocational, recreational, religious, or social interests. We all invest our time and energy in one way or another throughout life. When the children were little, we helped them explore their interests. If they wanted to play the piano, we gave them piano lessons. If they wanted to play football, we encouraged that. Why should this not continue in adulthood?

If your daughter-in-law has an interest in snow skiing, then take time to listen to her tumbles and her expressions of exhilaration. If you are looking for a gift, you might ask if there is anything in the sport that she would like to have. I suggest that you let her pick it out. Then it will be exactly what she wants and she will be appreciative.

If your son-in-law is interested in auto racing, I would encourage you not to make sarcastic comments about the stupidity of spending all day Sunday watching cars go in circles. That may be your honest opinion, but you don't build positive in-law relationships by making negative comments about someone's particular interest. If he is interested in football, I would encourage you to learn enough about football so that you can carry on an intelligent conversation with him about his area of interest. Your interest may not be in football, but I hope you have an interest in building a positive relationship with your son-in-law. Relationships are built by affirming the interests of other people.

I remember the father who said to me, "My daughter married a man from Tennessee. He was a hunter. To be honest, I had never been hunting in my whole life and had no interest in it. However, when he invited me to go deer hunting and promised me he would be sure that I wouldn't freeze to death, I accepted his invitation. It was one of the most relaxing experiences I have ever had. Sitting on the deer stand and listening to the noises of nature brought on a calmness that I had not experienced in years. Now I go with him every hunting season.

I continue to have no interest in killing a deer, but I really enjoy my experience with nature. And my son-in-law and I have a great relationship. Who knows, maybe some year one of us will actually see a deer!"

It is in the exploring of other people's interests that we often expand our own world while at the same time building friendships that last a lifetime. When you express interest in that which interests others, you are giving them the freedom to be who they are. And you are choosing to enter into their world. This is the process of building friendships.

If I were to choose one word to describe the foundation upon which this nation was established, I would choose the word *freedom*. And if I were to choose one word to identify the key to unlocking positive in-law relationships, I would choose the same word. Granting young couples the gift of freedom is the most fundamental choice you can make in becoming a good mother-in-law or father-in-law.

PUTTING THE PRINCIPLES INTO PRACTICE

Guidelines for parents:

1. Don't make your married children financially dependent upon you.

2. Don't give gifts they do not desire. Ask, "Would this be helpful?"

3. Affirm their interests by asking questions and offering encouragement.

Guidelines for young marrieds:

1. If you feel like your parents are trying to control your decisions, thank them for their interest but request that they give you freedom to make your own decisions.

2. Don't accept help that will make you financially dependent on your parents.

3. Don't presume upon your parents' freedom by expecting them to be automatic babysitters. Ask in advance if they would be free to care for the children.

7

ABOVE ALL, LOVE

*T*he ultimate key that unlocks the door to becoming friends with your in-laws is an attitude of love. By nature, we are all egocentric: We think the world revolves around us. The positive side of self-centeredness is that we take care of our needs—we protect and nurture ourselves. However, once our basic needs are met, we must learn to reach out to help others. This is the attitude of love.

The happiest people in the world are altruistic givers, not self-centered hoarders. Jesus said, "It is more blessed to give than to receive."[1] If you apply this reality to your in-laws, you will seek to enhance their lives. "What can I do to help you?" is always an appropriate question. Their answer will teach you how to express love in a way that is meaningful to your in-laws.

One mother-in-law asked this question of her daughter-in-law and received this response: "If you could teach me to cook green beans the way you cook them, I think it would greatly improve my marriage." She did, and it did!

It was asking the question "What can I do to help you?" that stimulated the daughter-in-law's memory of her husband's comments on how much he liked his mother's green beans. Since her mother-in-law was offering to help, she could make her request without embarrassment. If you want to help your in-laws, it is always better to find out what they would consider helpful rather than using your own judgment. The latter may be seen as imposition, whereas the former will be seen as an act of love.

Imagine what would happen in your in-law relationships if you began asking, "What can I do to help you?" You may find that other family members will follow your model. When families learn to love each other and express it in meaningful ways, the emotional climate is enhanced.

One young woman raised this question: "But what if my in-laws mistreat me? How can I love them when I resent them?" It is interesting that Jesus instructed us to love even our enemies,[2] and unfortunately, sometimes our in-laws qualify as enemies. When we are filled with hurt, disappointment, anger, or resentment, it is difficult to express love. But difficult is not impossible. With God's help, we can love even our enemies.

The process involves admitting your feelings but not serving your feelings. You admit them to yourself, to God, and perhaps to your spouse. But you refuse to serve negative feelings. To God, you are saying, "Lord, you know how I feel about my in-laws. You know what they've done, and you know how hurt I am. But I know it is your will for me to love them. So, I'm asking that you pour your love into my heart and let me be your channel of expressing love." God will give you the ability to ask your in-laws, "What can I do to help you?" Then in response to their answer, you can express love in a meaningful way.

Remember, love is not a feeling. Love is an attitude, a way of thinking, and a way of behaving. Love is the attitude that says, "I choose to look out for your interests. How may I help you?" A loving attitude leads to loving behavior.

The reality is that love tends to stimulate love. In fact, the Scriptures say that we love God because he first loved us.[3] It is his love that stimulates love in us. The same principle is true in human relationships. When I reach out to express love to my in-laws, something happens inside of them and they are likely to reciprocate. And when they reach out and express interest in my well-being, my emotions toward them begin to change.

Kevin is a good example of this principle. He shared his story with me while attending one of my marriage seminars. It seems that Kevin's father-in-law was not at all happy when Kevin married his daughter. Kevin was a plumber; his father-in-law was an attorney and had hoped that his daughter would marry an attorney or a physician. His father-in-law managed to be civil during the wedding festivities. But Kevin knew in his heart that his father-in-law was not happy.

About six months after the wedding, Kevin's father-in-law woke up one morning to find his front yard flooded with water from a leaking pipe. His wife encouraged him to call Kevin, so he did. "When I got there," Kevin said, "his yard looked like a rice paddy. There was water everywhere. I knew that somewhere in the line from the street to the house, there was a major leak. I turned the water off at the street and called my wife, Janet. I had promised to go shopping with her that morning, and I wanted her to know the situation. She assured me that she would rather I fix the leak for her parents. She invited the three of us to come to our house for a quick breakfast. 'Good,' I said. 'That will give time for some of this water to subside.' After breakfast, I went back and spent the next four hours locating and fixing the leak. When my father-in-law insisted on paying me for my work, I refused. I told him, 'That's what family is all about.' He was deeply appreciative."

At that point, Janet broke into the conversation and said, "Since that day, my father has never complained about Kevin. In fact, he recommends him to all his friends. 'He's the best plumber in town,' he says. 'You can't go wrong with Kevin.' I think my father finally realized that in today's world, plumbers are fully as important as attorneys and physicians. In fact, sometimes you can't live without them. As I see it, character is always more important than vocation. I think my dad would agree."

Kevin's act of love using the skills he possessed to help his in-laws stimulated a positive emotional response. Since that day, their relationship has continued to grow. Genuine love is seldom rejected, but someone must take the initiative to love.

In making love practical, two words stand out in my mind: *kindness* and *patience.* In the great "love chapter" in the New Testament, we read that love is kind and love is patient.[4]

LOVE IS KIND

Let me reflect first on kindness, which has to do with the manner in which we speak to people and the way we treat them. One of the ancient Hebrew proverbs says, "A gentle answer turns away wrath, but a harsh word stirs up anger."[5]

We make in-law relationships better or worse depending on how we speak to our in-laws. Loud, harsh words make things worse. Gentle, soft words make things better. When you express your anger at your in-laws by screaming at them, you are not loving them. Love is kind. When you listen empathetically and then share your thoughts in a calm and soft voice, you are expressing love even though you may be disagreeing with them. In speaking to them kindly, you are showing respect for them.

If in the past you have been quick to lose your temper and lash out with harsh, loud words to your in-laws, I urge you to apologize. You have created emotional barriers that will not be removed simply with the passing of time. Apologizing is the first step in changing your pattern of speech from harshness to kindness. In your future conversations, begin to monitor and change your pattern of speech. When you sense that you are getting angry, take a "time-out" to cool off. Then come back and, with conscious effort, speak softly to the person with whom you are angry, perhaps speaking as softly as a whisper. In the early stages of changing negative speech patterns, we must often exaggerate the change. When you learn to speak softly, you have taken the first step in learning to speak kindly.

Once you learn to speak softly, you are free to focus on affirming the intentions of your in-laws, even if you disagree with their ideas. "I can see how you would feel that way, and if I were in your shoes, I would probably feel the same. However, let me share what I was thinking and see if it makes sense to you." With such statements, you are applying the principles for deepening in-law relationships we have talked about in this book. You are, in fact, learning to express love with kind speech.

Kindness is also expressed in the way we treat people. Kevin did a kind thing when he repaired his father-in-law's water leak without charge. Random acts of kindness enhance in-law relationships.

However, kindness goes beyond simply performing acts of kindness. It also seeks to treat in-laws with courtesy.

Families have different ideas about what is considered common courtesy. Some families think it is discourteous to wear a ball cap inside the house. Some families think it is courteous to stand when a female enters the room. Some families believe that a man should always open a door for a woman. Then there are table manners. Some families believe it is discourteous to talk with food in your mouth and that courtesy requires the husband to seat his wife first before seating himself. Courtesy may be putting your napkin on your lap and saying "Would you please pass the potatoes?" Every family has its own set of "common courtesies." Becoming aware of these common courtesies and practicing them when you are with your in-laws enhances relationships.

Your spouse is the best source of discovering and understanding the common courtesies of his/her family. Take time to discover what your in-laws consider to be courteous behavior. Write them down as a way of reminding yourself, and seek to practice these courtesies. You will be taking positive steps toward becoming friends with your in-laws.

LOVE IS PATIENT

The second key in loving in-laws is patience. You've heard the cliché "Rome was not built in a day." This is true in relationships, as well. Patience must become a way of life. We cannot expect all our differences to be resolved overnight or with one conversation. It takes time and diligence to understand another's point of view and to negotiate answers to our differences. It is both a lifelong process and the heart and soul of relationships. We cannot build positive relationships without being diligent in the process of communicating thoughts and feelings, seeking understanding, affirming each other, and finding workable solutions.

Don't expect perfection of yourself or your in-laws. On the other hand, don't settle for anything less than a loving relationship. We must make room for momentary relapses. None of us change quickly and we often revert to old patterns. Failures call for apologies, and apologies call for forgiveness. When we are willing to admit our failures and request forgiveness, it will likely be extended, and our relationships can continue on a positive track. Love is the greatest force in the world for good. Kindness and patience are two of the most important aspects of love. Learn to develop these traits and you will learn how to become friends with your in-laws.

PUTTING THE PRINCIPLES INTO PRACTICE

1. Look for an opportunity to ask an in-law, "What can I do to help you?"

2. Can you remember a time when you spoke unkindly to an in-law? Have you apologized? If not, why not?

3. What acts of kindness have you done for your in-laws in the past month? What could you plan to do this month?

4. What "common courtesies" do you need to extend in order to enhance in-law relationships?

$\mathcal{P}$ositive in-law relationships are one of life's greatest assets. Living in harmony, encouraging and supporting each other in our individual pursuits, helps all of us reach our potential for God and good in the world. On the other hand, troublesome in-law relationships can be a source of deep emotional pain. When in-laws resent each other, hurt each other, or withdraw from each other, they have joined the ranks of dysfunctional families.

The seven principles I have shared with you in this little book have helped hundreds of couples develop positive in-law relationships. I hope that you will not be satisfied simply to have read the book. My deep desire is that you will earnestly seek to weave these principles into the fabric of your daily life. It will take time and effort, but the rewards will last for a lifetime.

Enhancing relationships is indeed a worthy endeavor. When you enhance in-law relationships, you are making life more pleasant for your children and your grandchildren. It is my sincere desire that this book will help you learn to listen, show respect, make requests, grant freedom, speak for yourself, seek to negotiate, and above all—love your in-laws. If you practice these principles, I can guarantee that your in-law relationships will be strengthened. You may even genuinely become friends with your in-laws.

If you find these principles helpful, I hope you will share them with your friends. They, too, are likely struggling with in-law relationships. I believe the principles shared in this book could help thousands of couples develop positive in-law relationships. If this happens, I will be greatly pleased. If you have stories to share with me, I invite you to click on the Contact link at www.garychapman.org.

❧ The purpose of listening is to discover what is going on inside the minds and emotions of other people. If we understand why people do what they do, we can have more appropriate responses.

❧ Relationships are built by seeking understanding. They are destroyed by interruptions and arguments.

❧ Affirming statements do not mean that you necessarily agree with what your in-laws have said. It does mean that you listened long enough to see the world through their eyes and to understand that, in their minds, what they are doing makes good sense. You are affirming their humanity, the right to think and feel differently from other people.

- Respect leads me to give my in-laws the same freedom that God allows me and all humans—the freedom to be different. Therefore, I will not seek to impose my will upon my in-laws. Rather, when I find myself at odds with them, I will look for a solution that will show respect for our differences.

- Religious differences often become divisive in the marriage. They can also create barriers to wholesome in-law relationships.

- The invasion of privacy is a common area of conflict with in-laws. But when the younger couple show respect for their parents' and in-laws' intentions and openly share with them their own frustrations, most of the problems can be resolved.

🖙 The mature person is always looking for wisdom, even if it is spoken by a mother-in-law. When parents and in-laws make suggestions, their ideas should be given due consideration. After all, they are older and perhaps wiser than we are.

🖙 Learning to respect the peculiarities of our in-laws is necessary if we are to have harmonious in-law relationships. In fact, if we were to fight our in-laws over every issue that we consider to be weird, quirky, or wrong, we would spend the rest of our lives in battle.

🖙 When we begin a sentence with *you*, we are speaking as though we have ultimate knowledge of the situation. In reality, we are giving only our perception. Such

statements come across as condemning
and will likely stimulate a defensive
response from your in-laws.

🖎 When you speak for yourself, you are
making valid statements. You are revealing
your thoughts, feelings, desires, and
perceptions. "I think . . ." "I feel . . ." "I
wish . . ." "My perception is . . ." All these
statements are valid because they are
revealing what is going on inside *you*. You
are speaking for yourself.

🖎 To negotiate is to discuss an issue in order
to reach an agreement. Negotiation is the
opposite of withdrawal and resentment.
When we negotiate, we are choosing to
believe that there is an answer, and with
God's help, we will find it.

🖎 We cannot force our in-laws to do what
we believe to be "the right thing." We can
and should make requests of them. If we
have desires, these desires should be
verbalized.

🖎 The greatest gift that parents can give their married children is the gift of freedom.

🖎 Love is not a feeling. Love is an attitude, a way of thinking, and a way of behaving. Love is the attitude that says, "I choose to look out for your interests. How may I help you?" A loving attitude leads to loving behavior.

🖎 We make in-law relationships better or worse depending on how we speak to our in-laws. Loud, harsh words make things worse. Gentle, soft words make things better.

🖎 We cannot expect all our differences to be resolved overnight or with one conversation. It takes time and diligence to understand another's point of view and to negotiate answers to our differences. It is both a lifelong process and the heart and soul of relationships.

Notes

INTRODUCTION

1. Genesis 2:24; see Ephesians 5:31.

2. Exodus 20:12; see Deuteronomy 5:16.

3. Ephesians 6:2-3.

4. 1 Timothy 5:4.

5. 1 Timothy 5:8.

CHAPTER 2

1. *The New Webster's Pocket Dictionary* (New York: Lexicon Publications, Inc.), 1990.

2. Exodus 20:12; see Ephesians 6:2.

3. See 2 Corinthians 6:14-15.

4. See Proverbs 11:14.

5. Exodus 18:17-19.

6. See Exodus 18:22.

CHAPTER 5

1. 1 Corinthians 13:5 (NLT).

2. John 6:66-69 (NLT).

3. Matthew 7:7-11 (NLT).

4. Acts 20:35.

CHAPTER 7

1. Acts 20:35.
2. See Matthew 5:43-44.
3. See 1 John 4:19 (NLT).
4. See 1 Corinthians 13:4 (NLT).
5. Proverbs 15:1.

About the Author

Dr. Gary Chapman is the author of the perennial best seller *The Five Love Languages* (over 4 million copies sold) and numerous other marriage and family books. He is currently working with best-selling author Catherine Palmer on a new fiction series based on *The Four Seasons of Marriage*. Dr. Chapman is the director of Marriage and Family Life Consultants, Inc.; an internationally known speaker; and the host of *A Love Language Minute,* a syndicated radio program heard on more than two hundred stations across North America. He and his wife, Karolyn, live in North Carolina.

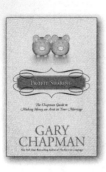

Profit Sharing

The Chapman Guide to
Making Money an Asset in Your Marriage

When YOURS and MINE become OURS.

Money is often listed as the number-one source of conflict in marriage. In this simple and practical guide, Dr. Gary Chapman shows couples how to work together as a team to manage their finances.

Now What?

The Chapman Guide to
Marriage After Children

And then there were three.

Relationship expert Dr. Gary Chapman answers the age-old question, "How do we keep our marriage alive now that the children have arrived?"

Making Love

The Chapman Guide to
Making Sex an Act of Love

"Let's make love." "Let's have sex." Is there a difference? You bet there is!

In his trademark simple, straightforward style, Dr. Chapman shows couples how to take marital intimacy to a whole new level.

Available now in stores and online!

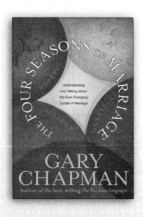